D0051663

The ADDed Dimension

CELEBRATING THE OPPORTUNITIES, REWARDS, AND CHALLENGES OF THE ADD EXPERIENCE

Kate Kelly AND Peggy Ramundo

WITH D. Steven Ledingham

A FIRESIDE BOOK
PUBLISHED BY SIMON & SCHUSTER

FIRESIDE
Rockefeller Center
1230 Avenue of the Americas
New York, NY 10020

First Fireside Edition 1998

FIRESIDE and colophon are registered trademarks of
Simon & Schuster Inc.

Designed by Brooke Zimmer
Set in Goudy Old Style
Manufactured in the United States of America

1   3   5   7   9   10   8   6   4   2

The Library of Congress has cataloged the Scribner
edition as follows:

Kelly, Kate.
The ADDed dimension : celebrating the opportunities, rewards,
and challenges of the ADD experience / Kate Kelly and Peggy
Ramundo; with Steve Ledingham.
p.   cm.
Includes bibliographical references.
1. Attention-deficit disorder in adults—Popular works.
2. Attention-deficit-disordered adults—Life skills guides.
I. Ramundo, Peggy.   II. Ledingham, Steve.   III. Title.
RC394.A85K44   1997
616.85'89—dc21   CIP

ISBN 0-684-83224-0
0-684-84629-2 (PBK)

THIS BOOK IS DEDICATED TO OUR CHILDREN,

*who have taught us at least as much as we
have taught them—about ADD, love, and life in general.*

THANK YOU,
TYRELL, ALISON, JEREMY, BRENDAN, AND CORINA

for the gift of your love and your presence in our lives.

ACKNOWLEDGMENTS

Of course, a book is never written by just one person, or even three. There are usually a host of other people behind the scenes, supporting the authors with the tasks involved in book production, such as editing, proofreading, and typesetting. And those are just a few of the many things on the to-do list as a book develops from the "I've got a great idea" stage to the finished product.

Aside from the concrete tasks, there are other, less tangible forms of support. As authors, we are grateful to the many people who patiently listened to us as we struggled with the writing process: the sometimes endless laments about deadlines, writer's block, computer crashes, and the frustrations of everyday life refusing to go away until the project is done. We also appreciate the contributions of those who listened to half-baked ideas and provided feedback on rough drafts.

We wish to wholeheartedly thank the following people for their help and participation in this project: Tracy Wright went above and beyond the call of duty, providing editorial assistance and compiling and formatting the first manuscript. Thanks also to Jody Rein, our literary agent, and her assistant Diana Lorang, for both moral support and careful editing. Maria Guarneschelli, Scott Moyers, and Jennifer Chen, our editing team at Scribner, have been endlessly patient and supportive, especially when we needed an extension on the deadline. Phyllis Heller, publicist for both this book and *You Mean I'm Not Lazy, Stupid or Crazy?!*, has been a tireless cheerleader, lifting our spirits with her absolute belief in us and our mission to get the word out to other ADDers.

And those are just the "official" helpers. Many others volunteered their time and talents to the cause. Kate's mother, Barbara Kelly, provided a listening ear, editorial help, and some "mothering" when needed. Kate's mother-in-law, Gladys Pentz, and Gladys's sister Sandy Noel reviewed the manuscript for readability. Thanks also to Mary Jane Johnson, Suzanne Belluardo-Cobb, Dorinda Dercar, Don Lambert, Bunny Hensley, Carol Webb, and Wendy Richardson for their support and feedback.

Last, but not least, we wish to thank our families, the ones we live with, for putting up with us for the duration. We know it is hard to live with us during the not-so-much-fun parts of writing a book. Thanks to Doug Pentz and Rob Ramundo, spouses of Kate and Peggy respectively, for moral support, some feedback, and even an idea or two. Our children—Kate's daughter, Tyrell; Peggy's son, Jeremy, and daughter, Alison; and Steven's stepson, Brendan—all had to "hold that thought" or otherwise delay gratification during many long work sessions. We thank them and appreciate their patience.

If we have left anyone out of this list, and we probably have, please let us assure you that it is a function of faulty memory and not a lack of appreciation.

PREFACE

Dear Reader,

When we wrote our first book, *You Mean I'm Not Lazy, Stupid or Crazy?!*, we were convinced that ADD was more than just a disability. Sure, the problems of ADD are real, creating much pain and suffering for both the ADDer and for those close to him or her. The difficulties cannot be denied, but they are by no means the whole story of the ADD experience. Our final chapter, entitled "From Obstacle to Opportunity," was a testimony to our point of view. We firmly believe that ADD brings certain ADDvantages with it alongside the disadvantages. Not only that, but the disadvantages have their positive sides as well.

We can't speak for everyone, but we do know that our respective life lessons have been invaluable experiences, learned in the school of hard knocks. Having a disability meant that we needed to develop quite an impressive array of coping tricks to get through our days and to work around our problems. It also made it impossible to take ourselves too seriously, because many of the situations created by ADD are too bizarre to do anything with except to laugh at them and at ourselves.

When you have ADD, the daily struggle exercises the muscles of your mind, and more importantly, those of your heart as well. You can't help but develop a sense of empathy for others with difficult paths, whatever their specific problem may be. The world of ADD support groups, conferences, and electronic bulletin boards is filled with examples of people going beyond their narrow concerns to reach out to others in need. It is a testimony to the human spirit that they are able to do so, even as they wrestle with the often serious problems in their own lives.

The interactions, however, are far from being deadly serious, most of the time. As ADDers, we use our gift for humor to lift the spirits of those around us. Our wonderful, wacky senses of humor, moreover, are just the beginning of a long list of the positive qualities we possess. We are creative, imaginative, sensitive, and energetic, to name just a few of our attributes.

Even those things that we are not particularly proud of have a plus side. Impulsivity, for example, can get you into major trouble at the same time as it gives the oomph to take the risks necessary for personal growth. All human traits have the potential to be both destructive and life enhancing.

This book is a celebration of the ADD experience. We offer advice on ways to modify the more extreme ADD qualities, but we don't presume to make judgments about the desirability of any of our suggestions. We want you to come away with an appreciation for yourself and the quirky qualities that make you unique, to value your differences and forgive your past mistakes, for they are just part of the learning process, after all.

During the writing of this book, we invited a third person to contribute a number of the entries, and we would like to introduce him to you. Steven Ledingham is an ADD adult who, like ourselves, is a pioneer in the uncharted territory of this relatively newly recognized disorder in adults. Steven was the founder of one of the earliest support groups for ADD adults, ASK—Adults Seeking Knowledge about ADD—in Dayton, Ohio. This group was not only one of the charter groups, it was also one of the best organized and most successful. Steven is also the author of two ADD-related books: *The ASK Guide to ADD Self-Help Groups* and *Scoutmaster's Guide to ADD*. In addition to his writing activities, Steven is employed as an

ADD coach, with clients from as far away as New Zealand! He is also a nationally recognized speaker on ADD issues, presenting workshops for employers and educators and training support group leaders from around the country. In his spare time, this busy person surfs the Internet, gathering ADD resources and information and maintaining a Web site. We are pleased to include Steven's unique point of view and his rich and varied background in this book.

And now, we invite you to browse through the pages of this book. We *do* mean browse. When we wrote the first book, we were careful to break it up into bite-size chunks, knowing that ADDers aren't overly fond of reading large, text-intensive books. This time we made the book even more user friendly, with a page-at-a-time format. You can read it backward, you can read it forward, or you can start anywhere in the middle. Don't think of this book as a heavy assignment to be completed in a certain way, by a certain deadline. Simply enjoy.

Yours,
Kate Kelly and Peggy Ramundo

CONTENTS

FOREWORD

In August 1994, I was traveling through one of the most remote regions of central India, sharing an ancient train compartment with an Indian physician and two Indian businessmen. Since we had twelve hours together and it was in the middle of monsoon season, there wasn't much to do but talk.

"Have you ever heard of Attention Deficit Disorder?" I asked.

They gave me a blank look and said they hadn't. Even the physician was baffled: It was something he hadn't encountered in medical school, or perhaps had forgotten about in his years of treating cholera, leprosy, malaria, and the other serious and often epidemic diseases that plague India.

So I described to them the life of a typical adult with ADD as I perceived it: the disorganization, the constant change, the job-hopping and often fleeting relationships, the attraction to independence and entrepreneurialism, the distrust of institutions and bureaucracies, both corporate, political, and religious. As I talked, they all nodded their heads: They knew such individuals.

"What do you call people like this?" I finally asked.

"We call them old souls," the physician said. "We have great respect for such persons." They told me that in Hinduism's scenario of reincarnation, as people move from lifetime to lifetime toward the ultimate goal of God realization, they often die with "unfinished business." When such a person finally is getting close to their last few lifetimes, close to enlightenment, they often must engage in a search-and-find mission to touch and resolve all those people and situations that represent little threads and left-over bits from previous lives. And behaviors characteristic of that mission, according to these men, are what Western medicine calls a "disorder." One of the businessmen laughed and shook his head. "You have very strange ways of seeing people," he said. "To mistake an old soul for a sick person. This is truly odd."

Odd, indeed. You are holding in your hands a book for old souls, written by old souls. Authors Kate Kelly, Peggy Ramundo, and Steven Ledingham are sensitive, insightful, caring, and "diagnosable" people, with extraordinary compassion and understanding for the special skills, insights, and challenges of adults with ADD. And so it would only be natural that they would write a book that answers the perpetual battle cry of the self-aware ADD adult: "What's next?"

What's next, of course, are celebration and self-realization. *The ADDed Dimension* is a celebration of life, the human condition, and all those odd quirks that cause ADD people to recognize one another instantly even in a crowd and know that we're all members of the same tribe. And in that recognition is powerful self-realization. If this book affects you as it did me, you'll giggle and smile and cry and laugh out loud. Over and over again, it threw me back through my life into lessons learned, pains survived, and joys relived. Celebration and self-realization: In this book they are the essence of healing and living. They are the essence of survival and growth. They are the essence of spiritual awakening and regeneration. They are the essence of Kate, Peggy, and Steven, come to think of it. Enjoy.

Thom Hartmann
Atlanta, 1996

The ADDed Dimension

I

Excess Baggage— The Shoulds: Blame, Shame, Guilt, and Other Useless Emotions

We pick up a lot of excess negative baggage growing up with ADD as our constant companion. Some of the problems we struggle with are a direct result of our biological differences. Many of our difficulties, however, are compounded by the experience of living our lives with a hidden disability. We don't know why we act as we do, and the people who observe our struggles haven't a clue either. It is in the nature of the human animal to come up with theories and quasi-explanations for phenomena we can't understand or control. In ancient Greece, for example, the gods were the culprits for just about everything people didn't like. It was a nifty system. All you had to do was please the gods, through sacrifice, or good behavior, and they would stop ruining your crops with floods and sending lightning bolts in your direction.

Of course, in our greater scientific wisdom, we know better now. At least we don't actually believe that there is a stern-faced God up there, physically tossing bolts of thunder at misbehaving humans. But we still have false beliefs, based on made-up and untested explanations for things that puzzle us. ADD is one of those brain teasers. We are just beginning to ask the questions and do the research that will lead to a better understanding of this complex disorder.

Of course, human nature being what it is, the lack of real information hasn't stopped people from voicing untested theories about ADD, theories that morph into axioms with enough repetition. You have no doubt heard many of the educated guesses that are presented as gospel truth. "ADD is a problem with motivation—if you would just try harder . . ." and "You can do it when you want to" are a couple of myths that come to mind.

As ADDers, after a lifetime of hearing and absorbing

these myths, we start to believe them ourselves. Not totally, because these "words of wisdom" don't quite jibe with our life experience. But on some level, we internalize this, and begin to feel that the problems are all our fault and that we could fix them if we worked hard enough.

We suffer from an enormous amount of self-blame, guilt, and shame as a result of false beliefs. Getting rid of these crippling emotions, however, is not an instant process. It is not just a matter of telling the people who spout the myths of ADD to take a powder. We need to search our own souls and examine the beliefs we have absorbed from our culture, looking at them in the light of new information.

"If it isn't the sheriff it's the finance company. I've got
more attachments on me than a vacuum cleaner."
                                          —*John Barrymore*

We hate to generalize about such a large group of people,
but we would venture to guess that most of us hate to be
tied down too much. Of course, it is impossible not to pick
up some baggage along the way, but we believe that we are
more sensitive to things that pull or clutch at us than the
average person. So, some of us go from one limited relationship to another, or avoid relationships altogether.
Others job-hop, or try out a million hobbies without really
mastering any one of them. We fear being dragged down
by the weight of someone else's expectations or becoming
trapped in a dead-end situation. But the result of merely
skimming the surface can be an empty and unfulfilled life.

A Way Around It—Do continue to monitor the attachments in your life. But realize that it is not really a numer-
ical problem, but one of quality control. Sort through your
commitments to get some sense of your priorities, and
then jettison some in order to do justice to the ones that
remain. Remember, however, that it is possible to travel
too lightly.

"Doctors think a lot of patients are cured who have simply quit in disgust."

—*Don Herold*

And many of us do. First, we discover that ADD has been causing us a lifetime of problems. Then we obsessively educate ourselves about it, finally presenting ourselves to doctors for help. More often than not, we have to convince them that ADD is real and that we have it, and then we have to educate them about its treatment. This is not easy, considering the role and status doctors have traditionally held in society. Many do not accept a patient's knowledge and experience when it conflicts with their own "expert" opinion. Their medical training probably did not include a course on "new" and "weird" diseases, and how to help and learn from the people who have them. And so we go around and around, looking for a physician with enough humility, patience, and time to work with us as partners in treatment.

A Way Around It—Be persistent. There are doctors out there who have emerged from medical school relatively open to their patients' input. If you can't find help where you live, go to the Internet for resources and referrals. There are a number of ADD Web sites available, as well as the many discussion groups available to ADD adults. And don't rule out going out of state for help. (See the resources section on page 255.)

"Consistency is a paste jewel that only cheap men cherish."

—*William Allen White*

When did we start worshiping the god of regularity, uniformity, and predictability? Having some of these qualities, some of the time, is a good thing. We all need to be able to count on a certain amount of familiarity in our daily lives. Otherwise, our psyches would disintegrate in the chaos. But a perfectly ordered life is not necessarily to be admired or emulated. True, the *terminally constipated* don't make messes, but they often don't produce much of value either. Creating works of art, inventing new products, and finding new ways of doing things all require the ability to tolerate mess and uncertainty.

A Way Around It—Build enough structure into your life to form a support system for your psyche. You will have those days, after all, when you need to get out of bed but you just don't feel inspired. That's when you can fall back on your routine to keep going. At the same time, learn to overlook the disorder that is always present when one is creative and determined to live life to the fullest.

"I flounced down the stairs, confident that I looked drop-dead gorgeous in my new outfit and that the party I had arranged to entertain my husband's business associates was going swimmingly. And then I noticed the looks of horror on the faces of the guests. Somehow, I had managed to tuck my dress neatly into my panty hose on a trip to the bathroom."

—*Andrea Little, ADDult*

This contribution is from an ADD friend whom we originally met on-line on Prodigy. Andrea never did get used to corporate entertaining. She was and is more comfortable in T-shirts, jeans, and sweats, like many of us. Part of it is the discomfort of the clothes themselves. Kids with ADD often refuse to wear certain clothes because they "don't feel good." The fabric or the seams are irritating to those whose sense of touch is ultra-sensitive. And we have talked to ADD adults who wear their underwear inside out because the seams bother them so much. Another problem is that it takes so much time and effort to organize all those killer outfits. The makeup, the hair, color and accessory organization. As if we didn't have enough details to take care of. Is maintaining a certain visual image all that important?

A Way Around It—Evaluate your options. Do you really have to wear clothes that feel uncomfortable and alien to you? Perhaps you could do your entertaining in a less formal way if that feels like a better fit. Have a barbecue or picnic instead of that formal party. Put together a wardrobe that is comfortable and versatile. Simple, washable separates in neutral colors can be dressed up or down and take you comfortably to a variety of settings. Men can often get away with a turtleneck or open-collared shirt under a sport coat for dressy occasions.

"Modesty is the art of encouraging people to find out for themselves how wonderful you are."

— *Anonymous*

This one is so hard for ADDers. Many of us come across as boasters and braggarts—not because we are grandiose by nature, but because we feel so invisible. We are so used to being dismissed and ignored that we fear we will disappear altogether if we don't shout loud enough to get someone's attention. So we dance around, waving our arms frantically, and practically stand on our heads to flag other people down. But, alas, it always backfires. At first they look, then they laugh, if we are lucky. Finally, though, their gaze turns away in boredom or disgust, and we are worse off than before. Invisible fools.

A Way Around It—Try taking your act off the road for a while. Spend some time in quiet meditation, giving yourself the affirmations you require. Then practice listening to others. They only want the same thing you do—attention. You'll be surprised how showing interest in them will draw them to you like magnets.

"I'm in a phone booth at the corner of Walk and Don't Walk."   —*Anonymous*

Is there anyone among us who has not uttered something similar? We can (and often do) have IQs in the stratosphere and yet still miss the most obvious and mundane pieces of everyday life. We can't give directions to save our lives, we forget our own phone numbers, and we put the paper upside-down in the copier every time. For example, I was thirty-five years old and a graduate student before I learned how to use the library (I'm not kidding!). To make matters worse, almost every time we get stuck at Walk and Don't Walk, there's some "normal" person trying to play traffic cop, trying to force us to understand or remember something we can't. It just doesn't compute. We feel "stupid" and "helpless" and full of silent rage, because we know darn well that we don't deserve those labels.

A Way Around It—Abilities and disabilities in memory and attention are not the measure of someone's worth. As much as possible, we should seek out and surround ourselves with people who understand this.

—K. K.

"I have been a selfish being all my life, in practice, though
   not in principle."   —*Jane Austen*

And so have many of us, though we didn't always know
why. We've wondered how we could be so bad-tempered
or ungiving. A secret shame burns inside. The shame of
knowing your actions don't always live up to your values.
A voice inside scolds: "You are sensitive—you know all
too well the power of a careless word. So how could you
have just hurled off that hurtful remark to someone else?"
And what about all those sins of omission: the kind words
left unspoken, the refusal to help, the seemingly callous
indifference to someone's pain? Ah! but we now know
that there is a perfectly good explanation for our inexplicable and seemingly inexcusable behavior. ADD is the real
culprit.

A Way Around It—Have you accepted the reality of your
ADD yet? If not, take time to grieve, moving from denial
to acceptance. Get busy educating yourself about your
unique ADD differences and their impact on your life.
Perhaps most important, live in the present. It is tempting
to revisit past inappropriate behavior—either blaming
yourself or excusing yourself (as in, "Not Guilty—I plead
ADD"). Neither is helpful. Instead, focus on your actions
at this moment. You have no control over the past.

"I don't deserve this award, but I have arthritis and I don't deserve that either."

—*Jack Benny*

We carry so much baggage and so many labels everywhere we go. We get so used to thinking of ourselves as lazy underachievers that we don't recognize our real accomplishments. Even when a chorus of people enthusiastically draws attention to our achievements, we think or say, "It must be a fluke, a lucky accident"; or, "If I managed to do that it must have been easy—anybody could have done it." Our self-esteem is often fragile from years of criticism, initially from others and subsequently from ourselves. And it's a long road to rebuilding a sense of self. A first step could be to follow Jack Benny's example and say to ourselves, "I'm not convinced that I really earned that praise or that promotion, but I didn't deserve to struggle with ADD either." There! The account is balanced. We don't have to feel guilty anymore. Further along in our growth, when we are stronger, we will be able to bask in our accomplishments without qualification. We will be able to simply say thank you when praise comes our way.

A Way Around It—If you feel that your performance in life doesn't justify the rewards that have come your way, ask yourself this question: Have I ever been recognized and compensated for the effort and struggle that accompanied each small step along the way? Probably not. So you see, it all evens out over time.

"Only the mediocre are always at their best."
—*Jean Giraudoux*

No one can accuse us of being well-rounded, middle-of-the-road, or boring. Our style runs from flashes of brilliance, of insight, to those ADD days when all the circuits are jammed and the operator is permanently out to lunch. On those "bad brain" days, it may help to remember that our minds are different, not better or worse, but more uneven and tricky than the minds of other folks. But these so-called normal individuals don't tend to set the world on fire, while we often have creative bursts of energy that work miracles when we are able to harness and use our gifts. The choice is not ours; we are what we are. But if you could choose, which would it be? For ourselves, we know we would rather struggle with quirky minds than give up our creative powers.

A *Way Around It*—Give yourself permission to stop worshiping the god of normalcy, of the even-keeled and even-tempered. Celebrate your ability to produce what you can when you can, and try to laugh off the bad days.

"I was born in 1939. The other big event of that year was the outbreak of the Second World War, but for the moment that did not affect me."

—*Clive James*

A baby is forgiven for this sort of obliviousness. After all, it is an infant's job to be self-absorbed. As an adult, though, it is embarrassing to realize that major world events refuse to penetrate your foggy ADD consciousness. For example, in the summer of 1969, at least two things happened that had a major impact on our society. I didn't have a clue about either of them. And who knows how many other earth-shaking things flew right by my fuzzy brain. I don't know. I am still playing catch-up.

The two events I am talking about were Woodstock and the first walk on the moon. I only heard about Woodstock because someone on a plane asked me if I had been there. I was wearing a dashiki that barely covered my behind, so I suppose it was natural for an observer to conclude that I was a card-carrying member of the Woodstock generation. In fact, it took months for me to figure out what he was talking about. I would have missed the moon walk altogether if the director of a theater company I was performing with had not called a break. He told us that we could take fifteen minutes to witness a historical moment, and then led us to a TV set to watch the action. I confess that I was glad for the break, and enjoyed watching the show, but it seemed very unreal and irrelevant to my life at the time.

A Way Around It—When you realize how much you missed in those prediagnosis days, the awareness can be overwhelming. It may help to view life before diagnosis as a kind of infancy. You couldn't help but be self-absorbed, any more than a baby can. So now we can expand our horizons a bit, slowly playing catch-up. But as with all types of change, take it a day at a time and a step at a time.

—K. K.

"It wasn't that no one asked me to the prom, it was that
  no one would tell me where it was."

—*Rita Rudner*

Or maybe it wasn't really a deliberate plot to withhold
vital information. As ADDers, we have all had the experience of missing important chunks of data while our brains
were otherwise occupied. We daydream in a meeting and
later find out we didn't hear a critical piece of information
related to our pet project. In social situations we tune in
and out; half of the conversation fails to register in our
brains.

   As a result, we say dopey things that seem to come out
of left field. The others in the group don't say anything to
us when we miss a beat, they just give us blank looks and
change the subject. And the worst part is that we often
don't know what we missed. How can we search for information about an event or happening when we don't have
a clue it even exists? When we experience this frustration
on a regular basis, it is natural to be paranoid, to conclude
that "somebody" out there just doesn't want you to be
included.

A Way Around It—When you encounter this scenario,
remind yourself that it isn't personal. Make a point of asking for a schedule or specific information about important
events for any group you are connected with. Then
promptly write the information down, preferably on a cal-
endar. If you miss a big event anyway, let it go. What else
can you do after the fact? Any other response only aggravates you and prolongs your negative feelings toward yourself and others.

"I'll go through life either first class or third, but never in
  second."

—Noël Coward

This boom-or-bust mentality is a familiar one when you
have ADD. That indomitable inner drive is programmed
to go for the gold, to focus on getting first prize. Nothing
else will do. Except that we all too often land on our
behinds, coming in dead last, or close to it. Why does this
happen so often? It's usually because our reach has
exceeded our grasp of the basic skills we needed. On the
other hand, when we perform well, we can really go overboard, putting all of our eggs into that one basket and
ignoring other aspects of our lives. This singleminded
approach to life is not our friend. It impairs our health,
relationships, and sense of inner peace.

A Way Around It—Allow yourself to be in the middle of
the pack in certain areas of your life. Take that intermedi-
ate class rather than the advanced one that's a bit too
challenging. It can actually be quite cozy in that mid-
range. You don't experience the humiliation of being at
the bottom, but you don't have to kill yourself trying to
stay on top, either.

"Even a stopped clock is right twice a day."

— *Anonymous*

Even on the worst ADD days, if we really put our minds to it, we can usually find at least one thing that we did right. Or, if we didn't exactly get anything quite right, perhaps we came closer to the mark than usual. The problem with finding that small speck of wheat among all the chaff is the discouragement that crops up to cloud our thinking. I've had more than my share of days when everything I touch seems to turn into mud, or something worse. That old Midas touch, only in reverse. My boss and my spouse send out hostile rays of irritation, my son balks at every turn, and even my trusty computer is unfaithful, refusing to respond to my attempts to make it run the way I want it to. Even so, when I am able to step back and review the day objectively, I can usually find a few small instances where I was able to make some progress, or make a difference in someone else's life. A friend calls with a problem and I am able to give moral support, or I find that I have finished some pesky task that I have been putting off, such as paying bills. Not earthshaking accomplishments, but little things that help keep my self-esteem afloat.

A Way Around It—When you encounter those "dog days," temporarily lower your expectations for yourself and your life. Put your dreams and ideals aside for the moment, and concentrate on the stuff of everyday life. Give yourself a round of applause for each mundane task you accomplish, and for each small act of human kindness. Also, don't neglect your need for extra support at those times. If you are in the doghouse with everyone in your household, call a friend for that pat on the back.

—D. S. L.

"I never blame myself when I'm not hitting. I just blame the bat and if it keeps up I change bats. . . . After all, if I know it isn't my fault that I'm not hitting, how can I get mad at myself?"

—*Yogi Berra*

The golfer or tennis player or other athlete who blames his or her equipment for poor performance makes for good joke material. They deserve to be laughed at when they make public spectacles of themselves with their childish temper tantrums. We can see right through those defense mechanisms, and we label them poor sports. But is it always bad to dissociate oneself from one's mistakes and failures? Truly, excessive self-blame does nothing to improve performance. And blaming others does nothing but expand the circle of misery. Why not pass the buck to an inanimate object? Even if it is only partially true or really quite a stretch. That club or tennis racket doesn't have feelings and it won't talk back to us.

A Way Around It—By all means, indulge in a bit of hostility toward your sports equipment once in a while. Call it nasty names and tell it how much it let you down. But do this in private, unless you want to evoke laughter from the crowd. And don't get carried away buying the latest and greatest sports gear, thinking that it will make you an instant star.

"A ship in port is safe, but that's not what ships are built for."

—Grace Hopper

For much of my life, I suffered from a painful lack of self-confidence and poor self-esteem. By the time I was six or seven, I'd already figured out that I was a loser but was damned if I'd let anybody else know it. I couldn't dare reveal my dark secret by being me, so I decided to be somebody else. Somebody who was clever and cute. Somebody the other children would like. Somebody who was worth something. . . . It was the perfect solution.

I became a terrific actress, a chameleon taking on whatever identity a particular situation called for. With friends, I was the entertainer, amusing my audience with quick quips and practical jokes. With teachers, I was the responsible, dependable student—a demanding role that I pulled off with the help of trusting educators who accepted my imaginative excuses for unfinished assignments. Later, with my educator colleagues, I was the leader, the chairperson of committees, the school social director, the ideal "principal's pet." And through it all, I felt like a fraud: competent, confident, and smiling on the outside, but worthless, frightened, and crying on the inside.

When I was diagnosed with ADD nearly ten years ago, there was another big part of me to hide. Not only was I still a loser, now I was a loser with ADD! Of course, this secret couldn't be kept for long. My husband told his sister, and as they say, the cat was out of the bag.

What initially felt like a betrayal became the catalyst for major, positive change. Perhaps the most important discovery was that I'd been clinically depressed throughout my life: I wasn't a worthless being; I only thought I was because the chemicals in my brain had been playing hardball with me. And I never even knew it.

A Way Around It—Are you hiding, afraid to reveal "all your warts"? If so, consider how wonderful it would feel to stop pretending. Start by learning everything you can about ADD and about your unique strengths and weaknesses. And then begin the process of revealing your true self by disclosing your ADD to a trusted friend. Gradually enlarge the circle of people with whom you are sharing your self. Take it slowly, one small revelation at a time, as your security and growing sense of self-worth allows.

—P. R.

"There was no need to do any housework at all. After the first four years the dirt doesn't get any worse."

—*Quentin Crisp*

This might be a good mantra to repeat when you find yourself becoming overwhelmed by the general messiness of your life—in work, relationships, and a dysregulated self, in addition to the more obvious, concrete housekeeping problems. This almost crushing feeling comes in waves, each new piece of awareness giving you a clearer picture of the debris. Alas, the pattern seems to come with the territory as we traverse the long road of ADD recovery.

Blessedly, before diagnosis, the mental fuzziness prevented us from the full impact of our disorganization. Even with treatment, there is no way we can tackle the clutter all at once, as in one giant spree of spring housecleaning. Instead, we, and the people we live with, need to find a way to survive the disarray as we work to clean it up.

A Way Around It—Take it a step at a time and a day at a time. Turn a blind eye to the problems that are not solvable, or at least on a given day or during a certain period of time. A good rule of thumb is to focus on your goals for the day, trying to keep them simple and manageable. Of course, those goals should be made with the big picture in mind, and then broken down into doable chunks.

"In the face of an obstacle which is impossible to overcome, stubborness is stupid."

—*Simone de Beauvoir*

"Wait a minute!" you say. "Haven't I spent a lifetime being
called lazy, stupid, or crazy?!" That litany of accusations
seems to sum up the life experience of so many of us. No
matter how many times significant people in our lives
shook their fingers at us, exhorting us to try harder, we
didn't. It wasn't that we would not; rather, it was because
we could not. It appeared to others that we kept failing
because we seemed to give up whenever the effort was
more than we were willing to expend.

Nobody knew the real story, of course, including ourselves. The "insufficient effort" theory seemed a plausible
explanation, so we bought it. When we left childhood and
adolescence behind, we were bound and determined that
"we'll show them!" We adopted the clichés we were subjected to: *Giving up is giving in; Just do it; If at first you don't
succeed, try, try again.* These gems of wisdom have always
been sound advice, right? Wrong! Unless you believe that
being pigheaded is an admirable trait. Think about it.
Since when has banging your head repeatedly against the
same wall been the mature and responsible thing to do?

A Way Around It—Knowing when to stop spinning your
wheels isn't easy, but it is essential for mental health. You
may not be able to change the nature of the task you face,
but you can decide to simply "give up"—at least for now.
The break can be an opportunity to reassess the methods
and tools you have chosen for your task. This isn't an
admission of defeat. It is a positive, healthy choice to
honor the self.

"Boredom, after all, is a form of criticism."

—*William Phillips*

Maybe it's time to stop feeling like losers because we tend to tune out at the drop of a hat. We all have at least one nasty memory of a teacher's irritated voice and the jeers of classmates rudely calling us out of a lovely daydream. But why should we still feel guilty for preferring our private worlds to the deadening drone of a teacher cramming a bunch of useless facts into our unwilling brains?

Our inability to concentrate may just have been a healthy response to material that was dull and irrelevant. Or to the use of methods that did little to stimulate the imagination. Unfortunately, we didn't leave this particular problem behind with graduation. As adults we need to update our skills and knowledge constantly to keep pace with a rapidly changing world, and teaching methods still leave a lot to be desired.

A Way Around It—Stop blaming yourself when your mind wanders during a lecture or conversation. It may just be a signal that the instructor or speaker needs to wrap it up or at least switch gears. Look around you—the rest of the audience may be nodding off along with you.

2

Coping with Differences

Most of the books written about ADD spend a fair amount of time discussing the differences in the ways our minds work—the differences between the way we function, neurologically speaking, and the way the "normal" mind functions. Not that we have any idea what the word *normal* really means, never having made the acquaintence of anyone who met the textbook criteria of a human being with a perfectly functioning mind!

Since it would seem that no one has ever actually achieved that exalted state of mind, whatever it is, maybe we should just relax and accept the quirky brains we have. Take a good look at what we have to work with, and figure out how to make the best of it. We were certainly given some odd, and often difficult, "symptoms" when God passed out the ADD genes. Much of the time, the advice given to us as ADDers is focused on how to work around our "symptoms," or make them go away. We all know, though, that they don't seem to go away, no matter how hard we try. And working around them all the time is exhausting.

Maybe we have been barking up the wrong tree, so to speak. Perhaps it isn't a matter of banishing or pushing around our differences, but of learning to make those differences work for us. The first step is to stop making negative judgments about how we function—now, right at this moment. The next step is to tease out the positive aspects of each ADD "symptom." In "Coping with Differences," we'll try to do just that.

"Don't tell me that worry doesn't do any good. I know better. The things I worry about don't happen."

—Anonymous

As ADD adults we often can, and do, worry about everything. After all, we have had ample experience with mistakes, chaos, and life accidents. We know how easily the best-made plan can take a sharp left turn, going its own way. Worry, however, doesn't really do anything to ward off the unpleasant events destined to happen in our lives.

The only purpose we can see for worrying is that it allows us to mentally trick ourselves. We imagine the worst-case scenarios, in gory detail. And then, when we manage to escape going to debtors' prison or having to defend ourselves in court, for example, we feel a great sense of relief. "Thank God!" each of us says to ourself, "I managed to avoid my personal version of Hell once again."

In fact, nothing has really changed. The real-life problems and situations are still in front of us, but they don't look quite so overwhelming now. The problem with relying on this mental trick is that it is a painful and exhausting process, leaving one with little energy for actually doing something about the real-life problems. And it doesn't leave much room for R and R either.

A Way Around It—Rather than a helpful mechanism, worry is a bad habit and one that is hard to break. It isn't just a matter of pushing the worry "off" button when you become aware you're getting caught up in this mental loop. It may be useful, however, to ask a trusted friend to assist you in putting some boundaries on your worrying. When you are in the grips of a terrible fantasy about what might happen, call on that friend to help you ground yourself in reality. With some objectivity to balance out your catastrophic thinking and some logic to illuminate the flaws in your doomsday *ill*-logic, you will be in a better frame of mind to act on those events over which you have control, leaving the impotent thinking behind.

"If you can keep your head when all about you are losing theirs, it's just possible you haven't grasped the situation."
—*Jean Kerr*

Sometimes it's not a bad thing at all to be blanketed by a thick fog. True, the fuzzy focus of ADD can keep you from getting a lot accomplished, and it's not fun taking the heat from others about your "laziness." But there are times when a blurry picture of life can be downright comforting. If you can't see all the problems in your life, you can't be too overwhelmed by them. Taking medication, therefore, is a mixed blessing. We're relieved to know that it wasn't our fault when we couldn't function very well before. But, as the fog lifts and we see our many problems clearly, we may quickly find ourselves in the overload and burnout mode.

A Way Around It—It's okay to take a holiday from medication, for a day or a weekend. A temporary retreat into the fog, where the demands of life don't press in quite so hard, can be a blessing. Your problems will still be waiting for you when you get back from your "holiday," but you may have more strength with which to deal with them.

"A retentive memory may be a good thing, but the ability to forget is the true token of greatness."

—*Elbert Hubbard*

At last! A positive slant on our leaky memories. But seriously, folks, there is an advantage to having—let's call it a forgiving memory. It's hard to hold a grudge when you can't remember what the fight or slight was all about to begin with. And what a relief it is to find that those embarrassing memories sometimes fog over pretty quickly. Much easier to forgive yourself your own trespasses when you can't clearly remember what you actually did last night or last week. You can't go back and fix it, so what is the point of remembering your less than stellar moments in excruciating detail.

A Way Around It—As long as you can recall enough about your detours to continue trying to steer a straight course, don't sweat the small stuff. And nobody, including God, ever said that we should turn the other cheek and keep coming back for more. You can forgive the sins of others at the same time that you try to steer clear of those who make a habit of hurting or abusing you.

"I'm not a fighter, I have bad reflexes. I was once run over by a car being pushed by two guys."

—*Woody Allen*

Even though I am a woman, and supposedly exempt from having to defend my honor physically, I can empathize with Woody on this one. Women, as well as men today, are expected to do battle with words instead of fists. Though I am a wordsmith, I have never had good verbal reflexes in the heat of an exchange. My thoughts drown in a sea of defensive emotions, and I am left speechless and humiliated, the victim of my ADD brain under stimulus overload. Naturally, the snappy retort comes much later, after the offending party is long gone. However, I have come to value this seeming handicap. Becoming paralyzed in the midst of a fight does prevent you from hurling off remarks you could live to regret.

A Way Around It—Rather than view a tendency to freeze during conflict as a handicap, look at the advantages. There is certainly nothing wrong with taking time to reflect, although we might wish this were a willed choice and not the crossed wires in our brains. Since it isn't, put responses into writing or tape them if that works better for you. Either way, you can say exactly what you mean in an assertive rather than aggressive manner. And you can choose whether or not to deliver your replies.

—K. K.

"Happiness is the sublime moment when you get out of your corsets at night."

—Joyce Grenfell

When you have ADD, it can take you half the night to just shed all the many corsets you wear during the day. We girdle ourselves with image enhancers, socially appropriate behavior, and heavy-duty impulse control. We say we do this to ourselves, but that is only part of the story. We are taught, almost from the cradle, that our natural behavior is unacceptable. By adulthood, many of our natural responses have been beaten, cajoled, threatened, and admonished into submission. True, some of those responses are better off extinguished, such as combative-ness and self-centeredness. But, alas, the baby is often thrown out with the bathwater and we find that our creative, life-enhancing impulses have been throttled as well.

A Way Around It—Take your corsets out of the drawer and examine them carefully. Try them on for fit and comfort. Take the whalebones out of the ones that are too stiff and throw away the ones you don't need anymore. Better still, go out and buy some sensuous, silky underwear.

"Humor is emotional chaos remembered in tranquility."
—*James Thurber*

Perhaps this is why so many of us have above-average humor IQs. Life with ADD may be many things, but it is rarely orderly. Chaos is the name of the game. So we use humor, one of our many survival skills, to make the proverbial silk purse out of a sow's ear. We have learned to turn pain and confusion into a snappy joke, complete with a punch line. Of course, this is not always an instant process. The pain has to set for a while, while we work it through and render it less potent. Then we can arrange it into the stuff for belly laughs. With more practice and experience, we can even begin to laugh, at times, in the moment itself. There is some consolation in knowing that we can make something positive out of all the mess.

A Way Around It—Discover, explore, and develop your gift of humor. We all have one, but at times it is buried under the burdens of life. In the midst of trouble, try to say, "We'll laugh about this tomorrow." With continued practice, laughter can become a delightful reflex. When humor rises from the depths of our beings, it can lift the burdens with it.

"Why did I write? Because I found life unsatisfactory."
— *Tennessee Williams*

Writing is so satisfying, especially your own story or a scripted version of it. You can tell the tale as it really happened or revise it until it is just right. Whether or not we actually jot things down in journals or become practicing writers, most of us do the same thing in the privacy of our minds. Lovely, fanciful tales where we get to be the hero or heroine. Or a noble, tragic figure. This is very healthy and affirming, as long as we stay grounded in reality and don't allow ourselves to become consumed by the fantasy.

Sadly, some of us put severe restrictions on our imaginations. Perhaps we were chastised severely for daydreaming as children, or have had our ideas shot down as adults. It is hard to shake off the mental restrictions that result from these cruel experiences. Whenever you try to let your mind take its own course, the fear surfaces—the fear that you will be wounded once again if you let your imagination soar.

A Way Around It—Give yourself permission to let your mind drift and wander once in a while. Talk back to any fearful thoughts or feelings that well up. Daydreaming is a pleasure that costs nothing except some time. Although it is not a good idea to allow your imagination to take you too far from reality, a bit of escapism is not a mortal sin.

> "Life is like playing the violin in public and learning the instrument as one goes on."
>
> —*Samuel Butler*

And life with ADD is never quite learning it, never quite getting it right, because parts of the brain refuse to cooperate. So we keep practicing, working to learn new skills and to improve the old partially learned ones. Unfortunately, we rehearse in public, in front of an audience that doesn't know about ADD, because it can't be seen. And those who do know are often skeptical, refusing to believe a real problem exists. ADD isn't an "explanation" for these folks, it's just an "excuse."

But they don't know how difficult it is to learn to play the violin, or acquire any skill when one has to work harder and longer at what comes relatively easily to others. Not to mention our feelings of embarrassment and shame as others watch us fumble and bumble our way to a better performance. Nevertheless, we are awed by the determination with which many ADDults approach life. Though faced with formidable roadblocks, there are still many, many ADDers who finally manage to achieve brilliantly.

A Way Around It—Your sense of humor and imagination can work wonders in reducing performance anxiety. When it's time for that piano recital, tennis match, or slightly scary social event, try using the old actor's trick: Pretend your audience (or opponent or new acquaintance) is stark naked! Try it now. Can you visualize those naked people? They're not so intimidating anymore, are they? Now you can focus on *you*, putting your heart and soul into your stage—or life—performance.

"Having children is like having a bowling alley installed in your brain."

—*Martin Mull*

The same could be said for having ADD! On the really difficult days, the noise from within and without is deafening. And if you add children to the mix, the decibel level can feel life threatening! Solitude helps a little, if we can manage to find some time to ourselves. At least then we have only the noise in our heads to contend with, those annoying intrusive thoughts and ideas. Some ADDers complain of hearing a constant buzzing sound in their heads. It gets much harder when the noise from our environment is added. We are sensitive to sound in the first place. And it seems that most children are dedicated to the task of generating as much noise as possible. ADD kids, of course, are much more intense and persistent in this task than others. If you have ADD, the chances of at least one of your kids having it are pretty good. So our home environments often come close to breaking the sound barrier.

A Way Around It—Survival depends on finding ways to turn the volume down. Exercise, meditation, and relaxation techniques can help you get control over a brain gone haywire. Don't feel guilty if you need to get away from it all at times—even from your children. Suppose you had a disability that required physical therapy. Would you feel like a bad parent when you took time for your appointments? Because our handicap is not so obvious, it can be hard giving ourselves permission to take care of ourselves.

"I assure everyone who thinks this is 'fun' [taking stimulant medication], that I will gladly give them all of my Ritalin if they will take all of my ADD symptoms too."
—*Milton Lucius*

The above quote was uttered in response to those folks who question the need for stimulant medication for ADDults. They say that we don't really need it, that we just need to pull ourselves up by our bootstraps, that we are just looking for drugs as the panacea to all of our problems, or even just to "get high." But we know better. We know that the decision to take medicine is a difficult one, usually made with a great deal of psychological struggle. We worry that it is a cop-out, that we are just not working hard enough to solve our own problems. And we do wonder if taking pills will be too much of a crutch. We hate the idea that we need to take a chemical in order to function as "normal" people.

Soon enough, after we actually begin drug therapy, we realize that there is no medical "magic bullet" that will cure all that ails us. For some, there is an initial flush of euphoria, not drug-induced, but at the realization that it is possible to live life without a constant layer of fog muffling one's consciousness. For others there is an acute sense of disappointment, when the medicine doesn't seem to work as it has for so many others. We don't need anyone to tell us that medication is just a helper, one that assists us in our own efforts to recover.

A Way Around It—Don't let the naysayers get you down. They have no idea of how hard you are working. They probably will not "get it" until it touches their own lives in a personal way. Keep in mind that no one should have to live with as much pain and struggle as we do without help.

"Whenever possible, our goal should be to 'march to a different drummer, but stay on the same parade ground.'"

—*Anonymous*

We know that we are different. Our uniqueness is a source of pain as well as pride. At times we suffer greatly because we fail to conform to the behavioral expectations of those around us. We become lonely and isolated, wishing that we could fit in enough to feel a sense of connection with the rest of the world. We feel like aliens from another planet, dropped here for some diabolical and unknown purpose.

On the flip side, at ADD conferences we receive an infusion of belonging, a rush of positive feelings as we celebrate our common gifts of creativity, humor, enthusiasm, and youthfulness. We sigh in relief and think, "At last, we have found a crowd that accepts us just the way we are, disorganization and all."

But then we have to go home. We find that the conferences and support group meetings are only a brief oasis in our stress-filled lives. The rest of the time is generally spent with people who don't understand and reject us when our ADD traits surface too much. So we're always needing to monitor and change our behavior with these folks in order to maintain a connection and a sense of belonging.

A Way Around It—Try to find a balance between stifling your unique self and "letting it all hang out." As a general rule of thumb, oddities are okay, but rudeness and lack of consideration are not. So when you see a look of disapproval, back off and try another approach. If nothing else, you will have gained more practice in the area of social skills.

"There is something wrong with a man if he does not want to break the Ten Commandments."

—*G. K. Chesterton*

What we are talking about here is impulses. We all have them and God must have had something in mind when he created us with the darn things. Who knows why? Perhaps to be the underpinnings of the life force, the spark that keeps the whole thing going. If we had no impulses at all we would never do anything, we would just stay comfortably stuck in our familiar ruts.

The trick is to learn how to be the master of the inner impulse, rather than its slave. We are all familiar with the general impulse to break rules. It doesn't really matter what the rules are, nobody wants to follow all of them all the time. Not blindly, anyway. And it is a good thing that we usually don't. Societies that become overly concerned with maintaining the social order often choke off their own growth. They eventually succumb to chaos, as people reach the boiling point and throw off the oppressive forces.

A Way Around It—It is important to find a balancing point between letting your impulses rule your life and clamping down too hard on them. No one can tell you exactly how to do this as it is an individual matter, requiring much thought and a lot of trial and error. But do try to honor your impulses even as you struggle to gain some control over them.

"The pencil sharpener is about as far as I have ever got in operating a complicated piece of machinery with any success."

—*Robert Benchley*

And some of us can't even master the pencil sharpener. On those more intense ADD days, I used to think that all ADD folks were mechanical idiots. With my limited understanding of a complex disorder, I would blame my abysmal performance on ADD. In truth, I am just not very talented at dealing with machines and equipment. You could call me mechanically challenged, as a matter of fact. The ADD certainly doesn't help, as it hinders my ability to endure the endless repetition that, as a slow learner, I need. But it is not the core problem, just another layer of frustration that I have to wade through.

A Way Around It—Recognize that ADD rarely travels alone. Most people have specific learning abilities and disabilities that help or hinder their progress in life. Help for your ADD can remove or improve one obstacle, but there will still be much remedial learning ahead.

—K. K.

"The only normal people are the ones you don't know very well."

—*Joe Ancis*

We know that everyone has skeletons in the closet. But we don't actually get to see them most of the time. And without much direct evidence to the contrary, it's easy to buy into the facades that people present to the world. They seem to have happy marriages, perfect kids, and to be so much more successful than we are. God forbid they should bite their nails or pick their noses or something. And we are sure that those others would cringe in horror if they actually witnessed the incredible disorder in our lives. Of course, we know intellectually that they have faults because they are human. But we don't always understand that emotionally. So, having a zoom-lens view of our own flaws, and an incomplete picture of others' foibles, we often assume that we are inferior or abnormal.

A Way Around It—Keep your eyes and ears open, and really pay attention to what others are doing and saying—not to find fault for the purpose of one-upmanship, but to gain a more multidimensional view of other people. Most likely, you will soon notice that they're not in any better shape than you are, and in some cases, a lot worse off.

"I think I can—I think I can—I think I can—I think I can—I think I can—"

—The Little Engine That Could

This wonderful, uplifting little children's book belongs on every bookshelf. It is a simple story with a profound message: Self-validation and positive thinking can empower us to overcome even seemingly insurmountable obstacles.

Despite inexperience and an engine ill equipped to pull a long train of railroad cars up a steep mountain, the Little Engine accomplished the impossible *by thinking that he could*. He made the decision to go for it, focusing on the task rather than on himself and his self-doubts.

In real life, of course, the ending isn't always happy. We can't expect to land a job with a salary of a million dollars a year simply by thinking we can! But within the context of realistic expectations and possibilities, ultimate success is far more likely when we choose to empower ourselves through self-acceptance and a can-do attitude.

A Way Around It—*The Power of Positive Thinking* is more than an overused cliché! We all have the memory of past successes to draw on when we need to access this powerful tool. Use those memories to create a personal visualization of chugging up the hill to your goal.

"It doesn't matter how slowly you go so long as you do not stop."

—*Confucius*

Many of you are probably scratching your heads over this one. "What in God's name are they talking about?" you wonder. "What does slow have to do with ADD?" Well, we know that hyperactivity is not necessarily the ticket of admission for an ADD diagnosis. And even if you happen to be one of the supersonic ones, does going at warp speed really get you anywhere? Or do you find yourself retracing your steps, painfully learning and relearning the lessons that you only skimmed the first time around (or the second or third . . .)? Our speediness is generally only an illusion that lulls us into thinking we are actually going someplace. With treatment and the awakening that follows, we become aware of how much we missed while living at that hectic pace.

A Way Around It—Sooner or later something will slow you down, whether you want to or not. You will need to reevaluate your lifestyle for health reasons, or because you can't keep all those balls in the air anymore. When you are able to accept a less frantic pace, you may discover that your accomplishments are equal to or even exceed those of the past.

"He shouldered up to the bar, after a month on the wagon, and ordered a double martini, with the proud announcement, 'I've conquered by goddamn will power.'"

—*Corey Ford*

Although we certainly don't recommend this particular method of working the first step of the famous twelve-step philosophy, it is true that you have to admit your powerlessness before you can deal with an addiction. As ADDers, we are vulnerable to all the problems people go to twelve-step groups for. Our dysregulated brains predispose us to struggles with substance abuse, eating disorders, out-of-control gambling, spending, and sex addictions. And many of us are used to dealing with our problems by exercising an almost inhuman level of self-control.

When you grow up into adulthood without help for your ADD, you have to exercise the muscles of the will constantly, just to get through the day. Those folks who accuse us of being spineless wonders who just need to buckle down don't get it at all. For so many of us, the task is not to apply more willpower, but to learn how to let go when a problem is too overwhelming to solve on our own.

A Way Around It—Letting go does not mean that you stick your head in the sand and order that double martini, max out your credit cards on a spree, or indulge in other self-destructive behaviors related to your impulse-control problems. It does mean that you recognize that you can't go it alone or gain control of your behavior overnight. Start with a visit to a twelve-step group that deals with your particular problem. If you struggle with more than one of these problems, start with a single one, the one that seems to give you the most angst at the moment. The skills you can learn in a twelve-step group can be used to deal with a variety of life's problems.

3

Emotional Roller Coaster

Emotionally, life with ADD is filled with ups and downs, sudden hairpin turns, and scary dips into unknown black tunnels. The good news is that all this action keeps us from dying of boredom. The bad news, of course, is that life on an emotional roller coaster is exhausting, and the excitement rarely compensates for all the stress we are subjected to.

Now, for the most part, this book is about the positive aspects of ADD, and there is an up side to our often dramatic emotional styles. You know that you're alive when you have feelings, no matter how difficult they may be to manage at times. Imagine your feeling patterns plotted out on a piece of graph paper, like the tracings of heart action on a cardiac monitor. When the pattern on an EKG machine, for example, is erratic, it means that the heart is beating too wildly to do its job properly. On the other hand, a totally flat reading means that something must be done to jump-start that heart, or the patient will die.

Feelings, those pesky things, are as vital to life as the mechanical action of your heart. They give our lives depth and meaning. Without them we are just like robots, going through the motions but disengaged from ourselves and others. The goal is to keep feelings under enough control without choking the life out of them.

When you have ADD, it is all too easy to fall into unhealthy ways of dealing with emotions. Born with temperamental emotional thermostats, our feelings can seem to be scary and unmanageable demons that we have to stuff down inside so they don't get out of hand. When we sit on them too much, however, they just get bigger, and they always get their revenge, expressing themselves in inappropriate ways.

In this section, we offer some thoughts and advice on how to whittle your feelings down to a manageable human size, so that you can experience them as the life-enhancing emotions they were meant to be. Not by over-controlling them, but by expressing them in ways that have a positive outcome for both yourself and those around you.

"If you do what you've always done, you'll get what you've always gotten."

—*Anonymous*

It's taken me a long time to figure out that nothing ever changes as long as one continues doing everything the way it has always been done. When something wasn't working, I believed that the issue was not what I was doing, but that I wasn't doing it hard enough. I didn't notice that the harder I tried, the more opposition I encountered. This often happens to ADDers because we tend to lock on to a problem and then lose our ability to see the big picture, including alternative approaches or solutions.

An example of a useless pattern I needed to change was something I call raging. When I ask my son to do a household chore he often gives me the run-around, as adolescents are prone to do. He gives me a million reasons for not doing it, or not doing it right away. He points out all of my imperfections and generally pushes my hottest buttons.

My usual response was to get sucked in, to engage in a verbal battle with my son until I was so enraged I couldn't think straight. Then I would start putting him down. With the increased awareness my ADD diagnosis gave me, I was able to step back and realize what a useless and destructive response my raging was. I have learned to take a deep breath, walk out of the room if need be, and approach my son when I am calmer.

A Way Around It—In a better frame of mind, I am able to listen to my son without reacting angrily. I simply repeat the request in a neutral tone of voice, without responding to his fighting words. This is in contrast to my old style of locking into battle, trying to get the kid to listen and comply by sheer force. In general, when you find yourself going around in circles in an interchange, back off and give it a rest.

—D. S. L.

"We should take care not to make the intellect our god; it has, of course, powerful muscles, but no personality."
—*Albert Einstein*

Most of the ADDults we know are highly intelligent people. Often, our "smarts" have been the only thing keeping us out of major trouble. We use our intellects to fast-talk ourselves out of a jam or to figure out how to deal with some mess we have made. So, we come to rely heavily on our brainpower as we maneuver through life. It has been our best friend in so many situations. Still, one of the big challenges for us is to resist trying to think our way through all situations. Logical thinking is only one component needed to deal with life's problems. When our intellect is totally in charge at all times we become machinelike, cut off from our emotions. We might as well *be* machines, for all the fun we are having. Our personalities become lifeless, stripped of everything that makes them interesting. We render ourselves stupid, in the way that computers are stupid. Computers can crunch data like mad, but they aren't very good when it comes to solving human social problems. They simply lack social and emotional intelligence, qualities more important to a life well lived than raw brainpower.

A Way Around It—Examine your typical coping style. Is there much more head than heart in the equation? If so, you need to rehabilitate the feeling side of your nature. Begin by trying to identify your feelings as you experience them. This is not an easy task, especially if you have been stuffing them for much of your life. Group or individual psychotherapy can help you if you get stuck, or don't know where to begin.

"He who conquers his anger has conquered an enemy."

—German proverb

Problems with anger and rage are quite common in adults with ADD. We can become "addicted" to anger because it increases the production of neurotransmitters that are helpful in coping with our disability. In effect, we get a small "buzz," similar to what a cigarette smoker might experience after finishing a smoke or the high a runner gets when he passes through the "wall."

I find it all too easy to get angry. It feels as if the anger is just impatiently waiting inside, desperately looking for the chance to jump out. My anger does not discriminate. It can explode at anyone, including young children, my friends, my spouse, or my employer. The reasons for my rage often seem pretty lame or silly after the fact. I have had to work extremely hard at learning to regulate my anger so that when I feel it ready to explode, I can do something more constructive with it.

A Way Around It—When you feel yourself becoming angry at others, consciously try to inhibit the tendency to lash out at them. If you can't control your reactions, get out of the situation. Take a break, take a walk, or go pound some inanimate object. When you have cooled down sufficiently, think about the reasons for your anger. Talk to yourself or write them down—whatever works for you. Before you reapproach that other person or situation, check to see that you are calm and that the issues are clear in your own head.

—D. S. L.

"A cynic is just a man who found out when he was ten
that there wasn't any Santa Claus, and he's still upset."
—*J. G. Cozzens*

My mother's been holding a grudge against the gas and
electric company for decades. It seems that sometime during the 1930s, the company failed to record one of her
always timely payments, instead sending her a not-so-
friendly reminder notice. Cynical of its ability ever to
change its ways, she's been holding a grudge against any
and every public utility company ever since! Her method
of revenge? She has never once in the sixty-odd subsequent years mailed a payment prior to the due date. She
showed 'em!

Silly, isn't it? Of course, who among us hasn't done
something equally silly and unproductive? But what about
our responses to the not-so-silly ones, those slights about
which we have every right to feel angry—the thoughtless,
hurtful behavior of an old friend or the betrayal of a colleague who took credit for your work? We may cynically
burn our relationship bridges, unwilling to let go of the
anger, choosing instead to carry the excess baggage into
our future.

Feeling things as intensely as many of us ADDers do,
it's easy for us to not only hold a grudge, but also to feed it,
adding emotional fuel to the fire. We feed off our intensi-
fying feelings of anger and betrayal, creating during the
process a kind of monster that ends up feeding off of us, as
we become consumed by the accompanying frustration
and stress.

A Way Around It—If you've been holding on to pro-
tracted anger about an injustice you've experienced, let it
go. The "rightness" of your position isn't the issue. The

real question is this: Whom are you hurting most by keeping a long-standing grudge alive? Nine times out of ten the answer is: you. Why? Because it takes ongoing effort to feed the "grudge monster" and keep the pain from the past as a part of your life now. It may make it easier for you to bury the hatchet if you keep in mind that doing so is really about giving yourself a gift—freedom from at least one stressor in your life.

—P. R.

"If you act like an ass don't get insulted if people ride you."
—*Yiddish proverb*

Let's face it, we all make fools of ourselves once in a while. Our ADD gets out of hand and we get overexcited, or we miss those social cues and say something that sounds really stupid. Our friends tease us about these lapses, trying to send us a message about our behavior that is softened with humor. Most of the time it's not such a big deal, but we can make it into one if we overreact.

No one wants to be around someone who can't admit it when they have messed up. The more we try to defend ourselves, the worse it gets. Either the ribbing escalates or the friends give up and go away, sometimes for good. It is so hard, though, to own up to those mistakes. We didn't ask for this ADD, we didn't cause it, so why do we have to apologize for ourselves so much of the time? We don't have the answer to that question, but we do know that it is easier simply to admit your errors and then move on. Defending yourself takes too much time and energy.

A *Way Around It*—Every so often we will act irresponsibly or make impulsive choices. Making the wrong choice once in a while does not make you a bad person. Accept that you may have goofed up and don't automatically get defensive when people "ride" you about your action. Once you have been teased about it three or four times, however, it is okay to say something like, "I admitted I screwed up, but I'm getting a little tired of this joking about it. Let's drop it, I'm ready to move on."

"What, after all, is a halo? It's only one more thing to keep clean."

—*Christopher Fry*

Maintaining a shiny image is so exhausting. Of course, we do need to do some basic grooming on the self we present to the world. Displaying all of our warts to anyone who happens to pass by could scare them as well as ourselves. As ADDers, though, we have trouble deciding how much of ourselves to display and what to conceal.

Being disinhibited means that we have the tendency to spill our guts to total strangers at the slightest provocation. Later, we recoil in embarrassment, worried that the information we have shared so casually will come back to haunt us. How could we have been so careless? Can we trust this person we barely know? Or even more to the point, can we trust ourselves? In reaction, the pendulum swings back and we go into hiding, presenting a false front to the world once again.

A Way Around It—It is a relief to let down your guard and share your human imperfections with others. And the more you do this, the more you discover that everyone's halo is a little bit tarnished. But how do you maintain balance in the area of self-disclosure? Number one, carefully observe the nonverbal behavior of the person you are conversing with. And two, tune in to your own gut responses. If you see, feel, or sense discomfort on either side, back off and switch to a more neutral topic.

"Don't get annoyed if your neighbor plays his hi-fi at two o'clock in the morning. Call him at four and tell him how much you enjoyed it."

—*Anonymous*

Ah! Sweet revenge for the noise intolerant. And a good ploy to remember for dealing with a variety of insults to the psyche. However, full frontal assault does not generally get us very far in dealing with insensitive people. It would probably be more effective to call your neighbor at a reasonable hour. And, with humor, let him know what you were contemplating in the middle of the night. For one thing, our anger renders us inarticulate and we end up looking like fuming fools. Or we evoke such a strong defensive reaction that we find ourselves embroiled in an endless war of strike and retaliation. Exciting, at times, but ultimately damaging as we waste precious time in battles that get more and more childish as they escalate.

A Way Around It—Use humor and good timing rather than hostility to fight your battles. If your foe is relaxed and can laugh as he or she hears your message, you are more likely to stop a vicious cycle of attack and counterattack before it starts.

"If they liked you, they didn't applaud—they just let you live."

—*Bob Hope*

We don't know about you, but that more or less summarizes our life experiences. Sweating and working like the devil to keep your performance up to par, and the only reward much of the time is mere survival. Frenetically tap-dancing your way through life, trying to shuffle along to a semblance of the beat, and making up a lot of the steps as you go along. But when you forget the steps, why, oh why, does there always have to be an audience? Most of the time, there is no one around to see your brilliant days when you produce your best. If there is, rarely do they jump up and give you a standing ovation. Yet there seems to be someone around to get the hook and drag you off the stage whenever you stumble and fall flat on your face.

A Way Around It—Try to move away from the performance metaphor in your daily life. Give yourself your own accolades and critiques. At the same time, attempt to block out that distracting Greek chorus of detractors.

"Puritanism: the haunting fear that someone, somewhere, may be happy."

—*H. L. Mencken*

Judgment and disapproval boil down to one thing—a simple case of sour grapes. Are these people party poopers because they fear the wrath of God, because they are too inhibited, or perhaps because they just don't know how to have fun? In their secret heart of hearts, they may just be dying to have a few laughs or a rousing good party. Maybe we should invite them to ours and help them learn how to let go. The frozen looks of disapproval might disappear if the perpetrators were included in the festivities. We're sure it will take more than a few tries to get a positive response, though. After all, people have a hard time loosening up after years of holding it in.

A Way Around It—When you are faced with a look of disdain or disapproval, remember that more may be lurking behind that frigid exterior than meets the eye. Try to ignore the behavior and work under the assumption that the "stiffs" of this world just want to have fun like the rest of us.

"The advantage of being ADD is you never stay focused on one thing long enough to get depressed."

—*Don Taylor, ADDult*

Wandering minds and poor memories have their advantages. When you have ADD, it is possible to have the day from Hell, only to wake up the next morning having forgotten the whole thing. A pleasant dream or lovely weather can wipe the slate completely clean, at least temporarily. Your distractibility means that you can be quickly pulled away from gloomy thoughts by something better that catches your eye and mind. You may appear rude, at times, but at least you are able to escape a certain amount of unpleasantness. In a world so full of conflict and seemingly unsolvable problems, the fickle ADD mind can give us an edge, one we sometimes need, in terms of staying afloat.

A Way Around It—Every characteristic has its positive and negative attributes. Try to honor the advantages of having a butterfly mind. It is one of the many things we can be grateful for.

"I don't drink and I don't take drugs. Don't applaud that! If I got shitfaced I'd probably start talking about insurance premiums."

—*Bobcat Goldthwaite*

Believe it or not, some folk secretly suffer from ADD-envy. It's true, controlled and inhibited people often long for a bit of our derring-do and devil-may-care attitude. After a local radio interview Peggy and Kate did, Kate's husband reported the following anecdote: "We were all listening to you on the radio at the office. After the show, various people enthusiastically reacted to it, but I noticed that the secretary looked pensive. I asked her what she thought and she wistfully replied that she wished she had ADD because we seemed to be having so much fun."

She was right, we do have fun. One of the reasons the radio interviews go so well is that we are willing to let our hair down and enjoy being ourselves—a gift of ADD spontaneity. But we have to get over the hump of shame and secrecy about our disorder before we can share our experiences in ways that are both entertaining and healing for ourselves and our listeners. And we don't have to get shitfaced to do it. We are very good at attaining a natural high. The issue we struggle with instead is finding enough balance to keep our natural highs from getting out of control, without being wet blankets.

A Way Around It—Your high animal spirits are a gift to be treasured. They need only a bit of domestication, not rigid and punitive obedience training. If you appear to be drunk or otherwise intoxicated, even when you have not indulged, you have slid over the line into the out-of-control zone. But it is okay to be zany, silly, or goofy, as long as it jibes with the mood of the people you are with. Above all, take care not to hurt anyone, with sarcasm or other types of humor that really mask hostility.

"He who threatens is afraid."

—*French proverb*

I often feel threatened by people who I believe have some power over me, or who seem to be trying to control my behavior. I think that this fear is a result of my experiences as an ADD child. When I was small, there seemed to be all these giant, powerful people around, forever punishing me and attempting to control my ADD symptoms. Back then, I was not aware that those adults were just trying to help me. They didn't go about it in the best way, but I now believe that they were just trying to help me gain some kind of control over myself. My parents and teachers looked all-powerful to me, but in reality they were just as scared as I was, afraid that I would come to harm if I persisted in my wilder ways.

I know that I now threaten others at times, but my bullying is just a defense, designed to hide the fact that I am terrified. I am afraid of losing something, someone, or my freedom to be creative. I may be afraid of having to change or learn new skills that won't be mastered without a lot of blood, sweat, and tears. Most of all, I am scared to death that someone will find out about my ADD and how vulnerable I feel.

A Way Around It—You may have learned threatening behavior at your mother's knee, but that doesn't mean it is a helpful way to deal with your feelings today. It may seem to be a pretty risky thing to do, but dropping your defenses is often the best tactic. Of course, you have to pick and choose the people you share your vulnerable self with, but revealing your true self is the only way to build close and trusting relationships.

—D. S. L.

"I was going to buy a copy of *The Power of Positive Thinking,* and then I thought: What the hell good would that do?"

—*Ronnie Shakes*

Much has been written about pie-in-the-sky ADD optimism. We often are portrayed as enthusiastic Pollyannas, with eyes firmly fixed on a silver lining. People see us refusing to acknowledge our stumbling blocks even while we trip over them. Some of us do play out this role perfectly, generally because we find it too painful to deal with so many thorny problems. We refuse to deal with reality when the bills pile up, believing that someone or something will bail us out, while doing nothing to change our spending habits. But others become professional pessimists, unable to block out difficult realities or memories of painful failures. Still others, perhaps the majority, swing back and forth between the extremes of optimism and pessimism.

A Way Around It—Sinking into pessimism, although it is understandable at times, is not the answer. Neither is a life spent sticking your head in the sand. If you find that your thinking patterns tend to settle into one of these two extremes, seek out people who have the opposite style. You may irritate each other at times, but you may also find a better balance in your way of viewing your world.

"I suppose one of the reasons why I grew up feeling the
 need to cause laughter was perpetual fear of being its
 unwitting object."

—*Clive James*

We believe that this is the primary motivation for ADDers
who carve out a role as the perpetual class clown. Of
course, many of us have special gifts in the area of humor.
We think most ADDers do, and a few of us can even make
a living performing stand-up comedy. Among the audience, though, the laughter fades when the routine never
stops. When one does a comedy act in every situation, it
becomes apparent that the jokes are just a means of keeping other people at a distance. If we keep 'em laughing, we
think, we can hide our insecurities. If we are the first to
poke fun at ourselves, we will beat other people to the
punch.

A Way Around It—By all means, enjoy the gift of laughter. But spend some private time examining the reasons for
your humor behavior. If you find that you habitually use
humor as a defense, try dropping "the act" in certain situations. Sincerely share your thoughts and feelings, rather
than turning them into a joke.

"Keep falling on your face—when the fall doesn't hurt anymore you're there."

—*Hattie Hill-Storks*

Recently I went roller-skating with my daughter, who retracted her request that I skate next to her after she watched my wretched performance for a while. Now, I didn't think I was doing so badly for a fortyish woman who hadn't donned a pair of skates for a couple of decades. I suppose that in Alison's judgment, however, I was a menace on wheels, threatening to take her down with me on those bruising falls. I am proud to report, though, that despite the wounding of my body and pride, I lived to tell about it. And I even managed to call forth old muscle memories, finishing the day with speed skating and a few fancy turns.

Falling repeatedly on your face isn't fun. It hurts. It's discouraging. It's embarrassing. Assuming, however, that you aren't being a glutton for punishment and pushing yourself way beyond your limits, the falling and failing are necessary. It's just an emotional low point in the cycle of learning. You can move beyond it and the discomfort of feeling like a foolish buffoon.

But let's not kid ourselves. The road to mastery is littered with embarrassment and frustration. Although that's the way it is for everybody, it can be a particularly grueling journey for those of us who have spent years wearing dunce caps and dodging the jeers of those who seemed to be using us for target practice.

A Way Around It—Nobody ever said that "getting there" would be easy. And keep in mind that even when you get wherever *there* is, there will be setbacks. You will fall less often and less painfully, experiencing far less of an emotional beating, if you're careful about choosing where it is you want to go. And that means figuring out and then following *your* agenda, not someone else's.

—P. R.

"Trust in Allah, but tie your camel."

—Arabian proverb

Many of us, against all odds, end up at midlife strangely innocent, as trusting and naive as little children. One would think that all the hard knocks and disappointments would make us bitter and suspicious, but it doesn't seem to work that way. Perhaps it is that protective ADD fog at work again, cushioning the blows and allowing us to forget the last humiliation or failure. So that, fresh as a daisy, we can pick ourselves up and greet the next challenge with enthusiasm. Or at least with less dread. But the fog may prevent us from taking safety precautions and doing the detail work necessary to reach our goals.

A *Way Around It*—When the fog lifts with treatment, we can become downright paranoid for a time. Work on your ability to handle details, but do it at a pace that is comfortable for you. In time, your trust and confidence will return, this time with a firmer foundation.

"There are some things it's good to have a healthy fear of—drinking poisons, leaping off tall buildings, sex with gorillas."

—*John-Roger*

Over and over again, we find descriptions of ADDers that portray us as major risk takers, daredevils who spend all our waking hours jumping out of planes, climbing up sheer cliffs, and racing our cars on the highway. For many of us, though, that image of ADD behavior is an alien concept. We look at our daily lives and wonder if we really belong in the club, because we know that we have become fearful creatures, afraid that our wandering attention will cause a major misstep or an accident. Perhaps we used to love skiing, but we gave it up after a bout of woolgathering on the slopes caused a close and painful encounter with a tree. We may have been full of beans as children, but the harsh consequences of our rash actions have been hammered home by the time we reach maturity.

A Way Around It—Don't despair; major risk taking is not required for a diagnosis of ADD. ADD is, at its core, a difference in attention, and not necessarily a matter of hyperactivity or risky endeavors. Some of us were born cautious, and others have learned to be careful in the school of hard knocks. Perhaps you will begin to take small risks and try new skills when your attention is improved with treatment, but there is nothing wrong with taking slow and tentative steps when you are venturing out into new territory.

"Grieving must be done in its own time. To deny the human reality that pain hurts only delays the process."
—*John-Roger*

When I first found out that I had ADD, seven years ago, the relief of knowing there was a reason for my struggles was short-lived. Shortly after diagnosis, I started on a wild emotional journey that lasted for about six months. My hairy ride was a thing that has been labeled "the grief process" by folks in the mental health business. "Well," I thought, "I'm in that business too, and I know all about it—it's a good thing, and it won't last forever. All you have to do is hang in there until it's over." So, I did my grief work, like a good little do-be. I wept and raged and fumed for months on end, and then, thank God, I was done. At least I thought I was at the time. I felt better than I did before diagnosis and was on a fairly even emotional keel.

Then I began the work of writing *You Mean I'm Not Lazy, Stupid or Crazy?!* I thought I was all done and ready to tell other people how to negotiate the rough seas of ADD. That was only partially true, because I knew the answers well enough to write them down, but I did not yet have the ability to practice what I preached. The road to recovery from ADD is a long and rocky one, with new insights leading to more change, and thus more upheaval.

A Way Around It—The life changes you will undergo as a result of an ADD diagnosis are monumental. It will take years, not months, to integrate all the new information and make the needed changes in your life. The emotional upheaval that accompanies this work comes in waves, rather than being a once-and-forever event. There is no way to get around the pain and effort involved, but there are certainly a number of resting places along the way— after you master an important lesson, and before you go on to the next.

—K. K.

4

From Chaos
to Balance

D oes living a balanced life sound like an impossibility for someone with ADD? We will not even tease you by hinting that it is anything but hard work to reach that goal, but we sincerely believe it is possible to find a more peaceful and creative balance in life, and worth any amount of effort it takes.

As ADDers we are certainly not strangers to chaos. In fact, some of us seem to have adopted it as a preferred lifestyle. Oh, we don't really believe that anyone makes a conscious choice to endure the hell of constant bedlam, but somehow, we find ourselves in that metaphorical loony bin, unsure of how we got there and even more perplexed about finding the exit.

Of course, the origin of all this chaos is in our ADD brains, with their odd quirks and often gerrymandered circuitry. The quirks are the ones we were born with, and so is the wiring, for the most part. Some of the circuits, however, may be of our own making. Scientists have recently discovered that the human brain is much more plastic than they once thought. Stroke victims, for example, have been known to forge new connections in their brains with therapy, in order to work around the damaged sections. It is not too much of a stretch to hypothesize that ADDers, in a similar fashion, have developed some unique ways of "rewiring" a recalcitrant brain.

Now, some of these hypothesized brain changes may actually be quite adaptive—a new and improved brain, so to speak. Others, however, are probably just best attempts at working around a problem. In real life, they translate into old habits and ways of thinking and making sense of the world. Those old habits of ADD thinking worked, to a certain extent.

One possible short circuit in the ADD brain is the one that takes us from the recognition of problems to the action taken to solve them. Of course, this whole dissertation on circuits is just our theory, possibly quite farfetched. But bear with us for a moment.

We know about the problem with ADD frontal lobes—there isn't enough action in that part of the brain when it comes to inhibiting those naughty impulses. Voilà!—you take some stimulant medication, and now your frontal lobes work better. You should be able to think before you act now—right? But the brain is so much more complicated than that; there are all kinds of connections and interconnections going on in there. There are probably circuits of learned behavior that are not affected by sprinkling a little medication on the frontal lobes.

So, we have to make new patterns and connections, and they don't just appear overnight. In the meantime, we are stuck with a brain that has learned to jump at the first and most obvious solution to a problem, without considering and comparing the relative merits of several possibilities.

There are many reasons for the chaos in our lives, but we think that a big contender is the habit of always being so busy stamping out the little blazes of life that we have no time to think about a way to stop the conflagration. In the following section, we will look at some of the ways our lives become unbalanced and chaotic, and offer some strategies for working toward a saner way of life.

"The most dangerous thing in the world is to try to leap a chasm in two jumps."

—*William Lloyd George*

Have you ever felt that it is your hesitation holding you back, rather than your ability? You take a running start to jump over a personal chasm, only to find that fear stops you in your tracks at that crucial last minute. You remember the last time you failed, or hear a voice in your head repeating a negative remark someone made about your chances of succeeding at a goal you had set for yourself. Then you lose your momentum, and lose the courage to make the giant leap that will take you safely to the other side.

We all have moments like this. Instead of beating ourselves up, calling ourselves cowards because we failed to jump, perhaps there is another way to view those moments of hesitation. They can function as a reality check, a chance to see if our plans have a prayer of working. An opportunity to stop and say, "Did I pack my parachute properly for this jump?" Past failure may have had nothing to do with either ability *or* courage. It could have happened simply because the work of planning and preparation was neglected.

A Way Around It—There is no getting around the need to take risks in life, unless you are willing to settle for mere survival. The big leaps, however, are more than a matter of taking a deep breath, closing your eyes, and going for it. If you don't have the skills or equipment to be successful, you are just setting yourself up for a bruising fall. When you do fall, or find yourself hesitating at the brink of a major challenge, use it as an opportunity to go back to the drawing board, to check your plans for holes.

"Psychiatry—the care of the id by the odd."

—*Anonymous*

You have probably heard the old jokes about shrinks. You know how the story goes. They're crazier than their patients and their kids are nuttier than yours. Having spent a large chunk of my life working and socializing with mental health folk, I can only say that there is more than a grain of truth to this. Sorry, old friends and colleagues, but most of us have at least a few minor bats in our belfries.

In my experience, people often go into the field of mental health because they want to help themselves or their families. Now, this is not a bad motivation at all. Indeed, the very best therapists tend to be those who have overcome personal problems and then use their experience to enhance their practice. On the other hand, the worst therapists are also people who have their own personal problems. The difference is that the effective therapists have their issues resolved or under control enough to focus their attention and concern on their clients, while the other kind can actually do more harm than good.

A Way Around It—Most of us have been or will be in the market for a psychotherapist at one time or another. *Caveat emptor* (Let the buyer beware!) is the watchword. If a therapist is obviously in poor control of self or personal problems, move on and keep looking. Remember, you are paying them to take care of you. You can often get word-of-mouth recommendations from fellow ADDers at your local support group.

—K. K.

"Every so often I lose weight, and, to my utter horror and indignation, I find in the quiet of the night somebody has put it back on."

—*Lord Goodman*

How could somebody possibly blame somebody else for his or her weight problems? But it makes perfect sense to us. Our culture not only values thinness to the point of obsession, but it blames the poor hapless victims of the battle of the bulge. Why wouldn't they want to look around for somewhere else to point the finger? The fact is, we do not have as much control over our weight as many would suggest. In addition to individual metabolic differences, folks with ADD struggle with depression and impulse control, both enemies in the fight to stay slim.

A Way Around It—Do what is needed to maintain optimal health and peace of mind. Both a healthy diet and aerobic exercise are great for the mind and soul, as well as the body. But check yourself when you find that you're sliding into obsession about your weight, food intake, and exercise program. Don't let society tell you how thin you need to be before you can be happy.

"The dog ate my diaphragm."

—*Anonymous*

This is the explanation a friend's brother's girlfriend gave when she accidentally became pregnant. We laughed because it was funny, but also because it reminded us of all our implausible excuses for missing assignments and other general screw-ups. Sometimes they were out-and-out lies, attempts to avoid punishment and censure. Other times, the fantastic tales were the gospel truth, but nobody would believe them because they were offered after a history of exaggerations and defensive fibbing.

There is a word for this weaving of tales to protect one's psyche: confabulation. Alcoholics confabulate, usually because they can't clearly remember the events of the night before. So they make up tales with narrative threads that pull all their crazy experiences together. Some would call this lying, but we don't. Instead, we think it is an attempt to make sense of a jumbled and out-of-focus world, to have an answer ready when you are asked to explain yourself. We believe ADDers often confabulate. We are not necessarily trying to deceive. Rather, we are trying to impose order upon chaos, and present ourselves in a more coherent fashion.

A Way Around It—Continue to make up stories, but keep them to yourself. Use them for self-expression, entertainment, and processing your experiences only. Stop yourself before using them as excuses or explanations. After all, what is wrong with saying that you messed up? Or that you don't know why you did such and so. You may find that practicing self-disclosure will not only increase your honesty quotient, but it will also pave the way for others to be more open and honest with you.

"He that leaveth nothing to chance will do few things ill, but he will do very few things."

—*George, Lord Halifax*

As people with ADD, we can swing in either direction. We can be impulsive, take risks, and have wonderful adventures. Or we can retreat into safety, or at least the illusion of safety. It is all too easy to fool yourself when you have ADD because the traps and the pitfalls are seen through a lens that is off focus. When we are living on the edge, so to speak, we may be oblivious to the dangers, even as they lurk and loom around us—until one of them gets right up in our face and refuses to go away. Frightened, we go home, draw the shades, and listen to Kenny G.

But sooner or later, boredom sets in, and we are compelled to stimulate our brains once again. So we venture out, start a new business, move across the country, or invest in a new and expensive hobby. But perhaps this time we put a toe in the water before we take a headlong plunge. Taking precautions before the fact can make the difference between success and failure.

A Way Around It—By all means, start that business you have been dreaming about, but research it thoroughly before you invest your money and quit your job. The same piece of advice is good for any new venture. Know what you are signing up for! Honor both sides of yourself. Both the risk taker and the voice of caution are necessary to achieve balance. Balance is necessary to maintain a semblance of sanity, rather than going from one behavioral extreme to another.

"The trouble with life in the fast lane is that you get to the other end in an awful hurry."

—*John Jensen*

Many of us get swept up in the fast lane, driven partly by our own restless natures, and partly by our frantic attempt to keep up in a world where the majority don't have a hidden handicap to deal with. We crank ourselves up and kick our reluctant selves into gear each morning. The trouble is, we have to work so hard to get going that the force of our effort often pushes us into overdrive, a state where our excess energy desperately needs an outlet. At first, the surge of energy and excitement feels good. But so often we then find ourselves involved in too many projects and activities, without a prayer of juggling them all. Eventually, pushing ourselves becomes such a habit that we are unable to relax or rest, even when we are exhausted, quivering shells.

A Way Around It—First, organize and sort your priorities. If you want to get out of the high-speed lane you will need to drop some activities and cut others down to size. For specific information on how to proceed, read chapter 7 in *You Mean I'm Not Lazy, Stupid or Crazy?!* Build quiet space into your life and routine. Short, frequent breaks for meditation or exercise can help keep your drive and energy from getting out of control.

"Remember that a kick in the ass is a step forward."
— *Anonymous*

In my own life, taking a new and positive direction almost always comes after a whopping failure or an unbearable humiliation. It seems the only way I can learn is by slamming up against a brick wall. And it often takes repeated trauma or a serious concussion before I step back and wonder if someone is trying to tell me something. In my early twenties I endured several years of emotional abuse in a relationship that finally ended with my partner kicking me out. Although I knew this relationship was a bad scene, I don't think I would have broken out of it on my own. Afraid to stand on my own, afraid of failure, I had cast this man in the role of savior—which he definitely was not!

I had little money after the breakup, so I hitchhiked the 350 miles to my parents' home. As I stood on the highway with my thumb out, what should have been obvious to me all along suddenly became crystal clear. I did not have to live this way! On the way home, I took a hard look at myself, denying nothing. I began making plans to go back to school, to make a real life for myself. From that day forward I took charge of my life. Not that I never fail or backslide. But that particular hard knock was a precious gift. It showed me early on that the price is too high, you have too much to lose, when you give up control of your life.

A Way Around It—Try to view your failures as lessons rather than defects of character. In other words, as the old saying goes, make lemonade out of lemons. And I am not talking about trying to change your toadish partner into a prince (or princess). You can only change yourself or your own direction in life. Count the hard knocks as the cost of wisdom, something that comes only with time and experience.

— K. K.

"I'm living so far beyond my income that we may almost be said to be living apart."

—e. e. cummings

Financial planning is not our strong suit. We often live on the edge, making less money than our peers and spending a whole lot more! The greedy "needs monster" beckons, tempting us to whip out that credit card one more time. He hisses in our ear, "Come on! You can get them to raise the limit."

Before we know what hit us, we are overwhelmed by debt, hounded and driven by bills upon bills. So why do we do it? We often feel deprived and buy things because, after all, we have to work so much harder than everyone else just to get through the day. We should get some reward for our heroic efforts. Don't we deserve a treat? But it would be so much better to find ways of "spoiling" ourselves that don't ultimately punish us.

A Way Around It—Instead of shopping, give yourself the gift of time—for the simple things you love and never seem to get around to doing. For example, take out a book, a movie, or a CD from the public library. Or go out for a walk and appreciate the beauty of the day. You'll be much happier than you were when you were racking up debt.

"The trouble with the rat race is that even if you win you're still a rat."

—*Lily Tomlin*

Oh, the rat race! That endless, ruthless treadmill with no end and no exit. For ADDers, just the routine details of everyday life can constitute a rat race. The growing piles, the bottomless lists, all of life's little messes growing at an alarming rate, endlessly nagging for our attention. Then there is the mind-numbing, backbreaking race to keep up with the Joneses. Who are these Joneses anyway? If we could find them and manage to catch up with them, they would probably just work twice as hard to stay one step ahead. So what is the point? We have to ask ourselves if we really want to be like them. Let's face it, would you rather have 2.3 perfect children and "house beautiful" or be a highly evolved person? The answer is a no-brainer as far as we are concerned.

A Way Around It—Ignore the dust balls. Sing a song, paint a picture, or meditate instead. Fill your time and space with joy and beauty in order to avoid the rat-race mentality. Remember, the only reliable measure on the road to self-actualization is your own yardstick, not the world's.

"My bad girl has been undercover for years, disguised as a middle-aged mama who drives a Volvo."

—M. J. Johnson, *ADDult*

Many of us, men and women, have pasts that don't quite jibe with our current standards. We were too wild as teenagers, the kind of kid our friends' mothers didn't want them to associate with. We got into trouble drinking too much, driving too fast, and having too many sexual escapades. But most of us cleaned up our act in adulthood, scared by the lack of self-control that had taken us to the edge too many times. Now, we may feel like impostors, playing out our roles as responsible, respectable citizens. Who knows? Maybe we're still operating from the fear that those impulses are still there and they will do us in, unless we exercise rigid control over ourselves.

A Way Around It—You have learned better self-control from your days in the school of hard knocks. And since you are no longer an adolescent, perhaps it is time to loosen the controls a little bit, but in a safe way. Take singing or dancing lessons and allow yourself to be silly at times. Nourish the positive aspects of that youthful spirit.

"My whole life is in a constant state of disarray, and the
one thing that doesn't change is the workout. . . . If
you're feeling depressed about something, you get on the
Lifecycle and you forget it."

—*Madonna*

For some of us, vigorous exercise is our best friend. No
matter how bad or chaotic things become, we can always
count on at least the peace of total exhaustion at the end
of a workout. And we are often rewarded with the happy
calm of the athlete's high. For others, strenuous exercise,
particularly the kind you get at a health club, is an odious
ordeal—painful torture to be avoided at all costs. It's boring, it takes too much effort, and we just can't stick with
anything long enough to get into a routine.

Nevertheless, it usually helps when we can bring ourselves to do it. We all know how exercise benefits the
body, especially aerobic exercise for the cardiovascular system. But did you know that it is good for your ADD too?
After vigorous exercise your ability to focus and concentrate is often enhanced for several hours. Some people
who cannot tolerate medication have had a fair amount of
success treating their ADD with exercise.

A Way Around It—If exercise is a beloved part of your
daily routine, stay with it. If you are a member of that
larger group of people who are exercise phobic, try to find
a form of it that is palatable. For example, a dance or mar-
tial arts class can be more interesting than calisthenics. Or
just walk, ride your bike, or dance to your favorite music
in the privacy of your home. But do find a way to get up
and moving.

"I have problems flown in fresh daily wherever I am."
—*Richard Lewis*

This sentiment may not be as masochistic as it sounds. When our lives seem to offer little else but an endless supply of problems, perhaps there is some comfort in the illusion, at least, that we control the rate and flow of life's challenges. Everyone knows that we need just the right amount of stimulation to keep that adrenaline flowing, right? But we didn't really order those problems. No one really knows where they all come from. Some may be caused by ADD, while others have a different source. Some we seem to bring on ourselves, while others appear to be acts of God or fate. Whatever their origin, we have very limited control over what, when, where, or how many problems we have at any given time.

A Way Around It—Of course you didn't ask for or cause all your problems, but in any case, you are stuck with them. So it's better to take a proactive rather than a reactive stance vis-à-vis those pesky obstacles. Instead of whining or spending all your time looking for the culprit, ask yourself what you can do about the problem right now. The only measure of control you can gain is by viewing the barriers in your life as opportunities to learn and grow.

"I play a musical instrument some, but only for my own
   amazement."
                                    —*Fred Allen*

My father is eighty-four years old and has taken up several
new hobbies within the past several years—just for his
own amazement. Or more accurately, for his amusement.
Among the classes he has taken at the senior citizen's center are drawing, painting, and wood carving. He and my
mother are running out of walls on which to hang his
amazing Santa Claus and dog carvings! And to be honest,
he really is developing quite a skill at whittling.

   My father's talent—or yours or mine—isn't what's really
important, though. What is important is that we don't
restrict our activities because of fear of failure. So many of
us with ADD arrive in adulthood with a self-defeating
sense of failure and incompetence. More often than not,
however, we failed only in our inability to perform according to some artificial, arbitrary standard of success.

A Way Around It—The quest for excellence doesn't have
to be the driving force behind all your endeavors. Hobbies
and recreational activities are not frivolous time wasters.
They are an important part of the overall balance we
ADDers need so much in our lives. So what if you're not
the world's greatest ukulele player—if you like to strum,
just bask in the pleasant process of making music.

                                              —P. R.

"The world doesn't want to hear about the labor pains,
   they just want to see the baby."
                                —*Marcia and David Kaplan*

Have you ever asked someone "How are you?" and
received a lengthy discourse on his or her physical aches
and pains, the numerous mechanical problems of the
lemon of a car that cost gazillions of dollars to buy, and the
current status of the bankruptcy proceedings? Too bad you
asked, huh?

Sharing in the life challenges of another is an important part of being a friend. If you have had a caring person
who has helped you weather the trials in your life, you
know how invaluable the support has been. But let's face
it, no one appreciates being used as a sounding board ad
infinitum and ad nauseam. It's true that having ADD
means that we have to work harder and longer to accomplish things—the same things done by our non-ADDer
peers seemingly effortlessly. The danger lies in our using
ADD as an excuse for lack of follow-through. And this is a
trap that's easy for us to get tangled up in. When push
comes to shove, your spouse, or friend, or boss wants to see
results—"the baby"—having grown impatient with tales of
the pregnancy and delivery.

A Way Around It—If you're struggling alone with your
ADD, find a local support group—peers who share the
experience of ADD. Then, take action to view the reality
of your ADD as an explanation rather than an excuse.
Break the failure pattern by limiting the number of commitments you make and by focusing on results. Finishing
one or two things pays a higher dividend than starting and
never finishing many things.

5

Relationships
and
Communication

Everyone knows that good communication skills are essential to forming and maintaining relationships. Most of the conflict we experience as we interface with others is the result of the misunderstandings, faulty signals, and crossed wires of miscommunication. There are an astonishing number of books available, offering crash courses in communication skills, as well as seminars and workshops for gaining practical experience. And, of course, all the books on ADD tell us that communication is definitely not one of our strong points.

So, we take the hint and enroll in one of those courses, or go on a reading binge, trying to cram as much information into our brains as we can in the shortest possible period of time. Of course, we know better than to think that a lifetime of faulty communication skills can be banished overnight, to be immediately replaced by the good stuff—the real McCoy! But hope springs eternal, and so we head confidently home, or to the office, after completing that crash course, eager to test our newfound ability to communicate.

We are elated as we launch into our first encounter with another being. "Hey! This stuff really works," we think; "this active listening and checking to see if the other person really heard us is pretty slick." Well, it works for about five minutes, and then the conversation starts to unravel. "What the hell happened?"

We're not entirely sure about what happened, because we weren't there, but we could take an educated guess about some possibilities. Communication skills are essential to relationships that really work, but they are only one part of a very complicated picture.

Consider an interaction with your spouse. If you have been together for a long time, your conversations with each other, more often than not, are familiar transactions spoken largely in a kind of special code. You know how it goes: She says, "Did you take out the garbage, honey?" and he replies, "Not yet, I'm trying to finish this paperwork," to which she responds, "I can see the truck coming down the street." Simple enough, right? But underneath this rather mundane exchange of words can lie a host of meanings, and old stuff from past conversations. This couple may be adding unresolved conflicts from a past marriage to their exchange, or even resentments from childhood.

There are so many possibilities. For instance, she may be simply trying to find out if the garbage is out on the curb, with the thought that she will take it out herself if the chore has not yet been done. Or, she may be asking her question in a sweet tone of voice, while she holds herself in check, seething because that "lazy bastard" never helps out around the house (just like her no-good first husband or her father). He, on the other hand, may have barely registered her question, preoccupied with his paperwork. He could also have heard it loud and clear, but is operating from his own assumptions, that she is bossing him around, just like so many people have done in his life. Get the picture? And that was just an interaction between two people—when you add more, the possibilities increase exponentially.

Our main point is that relationships and communication are too complex for simple and easy fixes, especially when you stir some ADD into the pot. They are the areas of your life that will require the most work, and that will be the hardest to master. Don't let this discourage you, however. Progress may seem to be painfully slow and uneven at times, but the rewards are great. In this section we will examine some of the issues that confront ADDers in relationships, and look at some examples of the multi-faceted process of communication.

"You can fool too many of the people too much of the time."

—*James Thurber*

What really scares us is how easily we can fool ourselves. Like those times when we fall into the black hole of day-dreaming. We can lose hours at a time, and sometimes even whole days. We are convinced that we were actually with the program the whole time, while in reality we weren't really "there." This happens to adults with ADD during social interactions all the time. We are brought back to earth with a thud, when someone asks us a question and we realize we have no idea what they are talking about, because we checked out of the conversation a long time ago.

It's tempting at this point to pretend that we really know what is going on instead of honestly admitting that we missed something. After a while, however, the practice of covering up our lapses catches up with us. As we miss more and more pieces of vital information, we are caught in a web of deception. We feel stupid and out of it, and we have to fool ourselves as well as others to hide our shame.

A Way Around It—In general, honesty is a much better policy. Of course, you don't need to make a confession every time you miss a bit or a piece of a conversation. Nobody picks up on everything, and your companions will quickly become bored or irritated if you interrupt the flow constantly with apologies or questions. When you have had a major lapse into dreamland, however, ask for a summary of the conversation you missed.

"Some people have built-in filters that screen out the boos and amplify the hurrahs. Those are the people who never know when they're in trouble."

—*Roger Von Oech*

The idea of screening out the boos sounds fine to us. The only way we know how to survive the put-downs is to focus as much as we can on messages of approval. That is easier said than done. For one thing, we pay more attention to and give more power to the boos. It seems to take four or five times as many hurrahs to counterbalance their negative effect, perhaps because the boo-to-hurrah ratio was imbalanced when we were children. We heard far too many derogatory comments in the days before we grew up and were able to exercise some choice about our activities.

For example, as adults we can choose to stay away from team sports if we are lousy at them. When we were kids we had to endure the humiliation of being the last kid picked for the team. There was no getting out of that hated gym class. Our self-esteem took a beating and left us vulnerable to depression as adults. The dilemma now is to avoid sinking into depression without shutting out all feedback from the outside world. For we do need to know when we are screwing up so that we can do something about it.

A Way Around It—If you get consistent messages from others that you are on the wrong track in certain areas of your life, pay attention to them. They can help you improve aspects of your behavior that don't serve you well. On the other hand, refuse to absorb negative messages about your worth as a human being. The trick is learning to pick out and use the helpful hints while you discard the judgment and disapproval that often go along with them.

"Patience is the ability to idle your motor when you feel like stripping your gears."

—*Barbara Johnson*

ADDers are almost always ready and raring to go, especially when it comes to talking. We are impatient and have trouble waiting for others to "get to the point." For that matter, we are not especially talented when it comes to waiting for anything. We hate standing in lines, being in crowds, or sitting long enough to listen to a lecture. For me, difficulty with waiting ties in with one of my ADD patterns I call "forecasting."

For many years I missed big pieces of conversations without knowing it, because I would try to predict what the other person was going to say before they said it. I don't know why I thought I could actually do this, but I think I know what I was trying to do. I was trying to predict what was ahead so that I could come up with a response. I was rehearsing a bit in my head in order to avoid coming across as a conversational idiot. Of course, this strategy did not work. My anticipation kept me so busy that I could not hear what the other person was saying; in fact, I stopped hearing them altogether.

A Way Around It—Try to practice patience—both with yourself and the other person—in your conversations with others. It will help if you relax your attitude toward the interaction itself. Remind yourself that you are trying to communicate, rather than make a display of your verbal skills. If you miss pieces of what the other person is saying or don't know how to respond, simply say so. They will be so impressed with your efforts to be a good listener that your lapses will be forgiven, if not forgotten.

—D. S. L.

"I like talking to a brick wall, it's the only thing in the world that never contradicts me."

—*Oscar Wilde*

I do too, only my brick wall is usually a blank page. A number of years ago, I discovered that nobody wanted to listen long enough for me to share all the thoughts and ideas bursting in my brain. When I did get someone to listen, they had the audacity to interrupt my train of thought, sometimes right in midsentence! And not only that, they would question and sometimes shoot down my precious fledgling ideas before they were strong and clear enough to withstand such scrutiny.

After years of fussing and fuming over this state of affairs, the light finally dawned in my stubborn mind. Why was I expecting other people to have attention spans, especially for my half-baked schemes, that were far greater than the one I had to offer them? But what do I do about all my wonderful musings that needed to come out? Thank God I had been developing my writing skills, because they turned out to be a great vehicle for self-expression.

A Way Around It—Just spew it all out on paper. Or blather into a tape recorder. Nobody has to see it, or hear it, unless you want to share. You never know . . . eventually you may write something good enough to publish. Suddenly, rather than no audience for your ideas, you could have thousands.

—K. K.

"The right to be heard does not include the right to be
  taken seriously."
                                    —*Hubert Humphrey*

And that is a major problem for many folks with ADD.
We have great ideas, but we can't seem to communicate
them in such a way that they will be appreciated and used.
When we manage to pull together a rambling string of
thoughts into a narrative thread that can be understood
by others, it is often too long for anyone's attention span.
Our audience wanders off before we get to the punch line.
Or we come on too strong, talking too much, too fast, or
way too vehemently, forcing others into a hasty retreat.

   And sometimes, when we think we've gotten it all
together, we discover that our ideas are way ahead of those
in the pack. Either no one understands our complicated
way of thinking, or they can't imagine how to make practical use of our proposals in the here and now. Great
inventors like Edison were very fortunate. Edison had
both the gifts of a fertile imagination and the practical
skills needed to make his ideas a reality. Most of us are not
so lucky. We are either idea people or folks with the ability
to make things happen. The idea people and the doers
need to learn to communicate well with one another in
order to get anything done.

A Way Around It—Keep working on your communication skills. For more specific information on how to
develop those skills, read or listen to the audiotape of *You
Mean I'm Not Lazy, Stupid or Crazy?!* If your progress
seems to be too slow, consider that the pace may be just
right in the total scheme of things. In other words, by the
time you are able to package your ideas in both a tempting
and beneficial manner, the world may be ready to accept
them and put them to use.

"I wasn't allowed to speak while my husband was alive,
and since he's gone no one has been able to shut me up."
—*Hedda Hopper*

Here's a possible alternative to the biochemical theory of ADD verbal diarrhea: rather than having a defect in the system that serves to inhibit the excess flow of words, perhaps we have spent too many years pent up and ignored, our attempts at self-expression tuned out. Just because we could never get to the point fast enough, or our ideas seemed too far-fetched, doesn't mean we deserved to be silenced.

Often, it is not that we were actually being told to shut up, but that we chose silence over the humiliation of talking to someone who was not really interested in what we were saying. It is true that we need to find ways to express ourselves that don't confuse or bore others. But how can we learn if no one is ever patient enough to listen to us in the first place?

A Way Around It—Find a sponsor, an ADD friend with whom you can give and receive honest feedback. Practice listening attentively to one another, but tell the other immediately when your mind starts to drift or you're getting confused. Not only will you learn conversational control, but you will have had the opportunity to express yourself. The practice can also give you more confidence in your ability to speak with non-ADDers.

"Your friend is the man who knows all about you, and still likes you."

—Elbert Hubbard

That is why it is such a peak experience for many of us when we finally manage to hook up with a group of ADD people. We can let down our hair and share a wart or two, and they smile in recognition and empathy, instead of showing frozen looks of disapproval. Usually, self-disclosure is met with reciprocal nods or a chorus of "I've done that too." What a colossal relief after years of burying our shame with cloak-and-dagger secrecy. At last, we have friends with whom we can be real, rather than the impostors we feel that we are much of the time.

A Way Around It—Find a group of kindred ADD spirits, if you have not done so already. ADDult conferences and support groups are good places to meet them. And from time to time, be the first person to share a faux pas. The response you get will be its own reward.

"We sleep in separate rooms, we have dinner apart, we take separate vacations—we're doing everything we can to keep our marriage together."

—*Rodney Dangerfield*

This sounds a lot like the marriages of many of us! We have no trouble giving each other enough space. This is one familiar script for an ADD marriage, especially when both partners have ADD, which makes for a potentially combustible combination. It's so much easier to circle each other warily and give a breezy wave as your ships pass in the night. And it seems far better than wrangling and fighting and setting fire to each other's fuse. In the final analysis, though, this script needs doctoring if the marriage is to be preserved. Freedom may not be an issue, but intimacy certainly is. After too many years of noninteraction, you find yourself wondering, "Who is this stranger who lives in my house?"

A Way Around It—If this marital script sounds all too familiar, get yourselves to your local marriage and family counselor before it is too late. An ingrained pattern of many years will not respond to quick fixes, fads, or a do-it-yourself operation. For one thing, you will need a neutral party to act as a buffer, someone who can support both of you in your efforts to really deal with the undercover conflicts without fighting and blaming each other.

"We judge ourselves by our motives and others by their actions."

—*Dwight Morrow*

Of course we do! It is very hard to step outside oneself to get a clear picture of one's own actions. And how do you crawl into the heart and soul of another person? You can't, and without either of these abilities, it is easy to cast ourselves as long-suffering victims and other people as evil oppressors. The ADD blanket of fog blurs and distorts the scene even more, because it can be both protective and stifling.

Empathy for another requires a generous amount of maturity and security. It is an impossible task when you are suffering yourself. When it takes all of your energy just to get through the day, the blanket protects you from the additional stress of appreciating another's pain. When you are stronger, however, and ready to reach out to others, the fog is not your friend. It muffles and chokes you in your efforts at understanding and acceptance.

A Way Around It—Retreat to your fog when you need to, but do what you can to break through it when you are in better shape. Realize that ADD is just one possible piece of the heavy baggage that everyone carries around. Past conflicts and traumas also weigh us down. But the burdens can become lighter when we use our experience to understand the difficulties others are going through. When we are able to empathize with another person, we usually discover that the other person is not that different from ourselves.

"Y'know, when we're not fighting, we get along just fine."
—*The Rockford Files*

Venturing into a relationship is a lot like walking through a minefield! Hazards are hidden everywhere, just waiting for a trigger to set them off. One misstep and a blast explodes around you, leaving you reeling, bruised, bleeding, and wondering, "Why is this happening?"

We may try boning up on our communication skills, becoming frustrated when the siege, with no cease-fire in sight, rages on. The way a relationship plays out, however, has as much to do with *mind traps* as it does with good listening skills, per se. These are the thinking patterns that underlie individual *battle plans*—the scripts "written" long before the warring begins. Feelings from prior relationships create automatic behavioral responses within the current one. In response to disagreements, we pull out our respective "scripts," reading memorized dialogue, as it were. There's the Helpless and Inadequate Script—*I'm wrong*. And the Blame and Anger Script—*I'm right and you're wrong*. There are others, the most deadly, perhaps, that of Disillusionment—*We should just get divorced because nothing will ever change between us*. The danger is in the narrow range of options created when we operate without understanding this threat to quality relationships. With minds trapped in a turtle's-eye view of experiences—his or her vision having been reduced to just a tiny slit of daylight—each partner is able to see few options.

A Way Around It—Becoming aware of the sabotage created by your mind traps can free your thinking so that you can choose to shift your role from victim to observer. This shift can help you recognize that the source of most arguments is a matter of differing opinions and that opinions aren't commandments but simply perspectives. This homework assignment might also help: After each of the next three "altercations," jot down a list of the thoughts you were having while each was going on. Read your list, reflecting on any emerging patterns and identifying your particular scripts. The next time a fight starts brewing, you'll be prepared when a mind trap begins to ensnare you, and will be better able to choose to think and behave differently.

"I belong to Bridegrooms Anonymous. Whenever I feel
   like getting married, they send over a lady in a housecoat
   and hair curlers to burn my toast for me."

—*Dick Martin*

This group would be a life-saver for many ADDers. Of
course, we would need a chapter for prospective brides
also. As a group, we tend to be just as impulsive in love
and marriage as in everything else. But it's a whole lot easier to return the unwanted results of a shopping expedi-
tion than it is to heal a broken heart or a guilty
conscience.

   Our romantic track records would surely be a lot
cleaner if we each had a sponsor to call every time we fell
madly in love. He or she would know our unique profile of
unrealistic fantasies and expectations, and could adminis-
ter that cold shower whenever we needed it. Love is one
area where we should definitely take it easy. There is no
need to rush, it only gets us in trouble. We don't, after all,
want to collect too many speeding tickets.

A Way Around It—Until some enterprising individual
actually organizes such groups, we will just have to wing it.
Or call a good friend, one who knows you inside and out.
Make a pact to support each other in affairs of the heart.
For example, when one of you sees that the other's relationship is going too fast, help put the brakes on, without
nipping the budding romance altogether, of course.

"It was a mixed marriage. I'm human, he was a Klingon."
—*Carol Liefer*

Your non-ADD spouse may view this scenario in reverse, but it seems to us that many ADDers feel like they're married to aliens from the world of the straight and narrow. We have our little flaws and foibles, but at least we own up to some of them. Admitting to our ADD status means that we have the courage to reveal our imperfections. Our non-ADD spouses, on the other hand, often get locked into the stance that I'm okay and you are downright weird. It's easy for them to take the unacceptable parts of their own human nature and project them onto us. We become convenient scapegoats in the dicey dance of marriage.

A Way Around It—Tell the casting director to take a hike. We don't deserve the villainous roles that we keep getting. Call your spouse on the carpet if he or she always points the finger of blame in your direction. In fact, get rid of that finger-pointing stuff altogether.

"Basically, I believe the world is a jungle, and if it's not a bit of a jungle in the home, a child cannot possibly be fit to enter the outside world."

—*Bette Davis*

Finally, a bit of absolution for the sins of chaos visited upon our children. Who among us has not felt horribly guilty about the impact of our disordered and messy lives on them? First we pass our ADD on to them genetically, and then our lifestyles prevent us from providing that lovely, safe, structured environment all the "experts" recommend.

We have tried all the behavior modification programs in existence with our respective children, but they never worked because child and parent became bored so quickly. But more importantly, each of us know the pain of being treated like an animal at obedience school. And we don't want our children feeling that humiliation. So we lurch along, improvising our way through the child-rearing process.

A Way Around It—Perhaps we have not done such a bad job after all. The world really is a chaotic place, and our children will have to deal with it sooner or later. Perhaps it's better for them to learn the necessary survival skills among familiar people first, people who love them.

"When I found out that my daughter had ADD, it was like I was in an elevator at the top of a building and someone had cut the cable. I'm falling, and can't tell where the bottom is."

— *Anonymous ADDult*

Those of us who are parents get at least a double dose of anguish as we go through the ADD diagnosis and grief process with our children. With a strong hereditary factor at work, we may end up going through this two or three or more times. To say the least, we feel helpless and panicky, realizing that we can't save our precious children from the agony of our youth.

Our guess is that not many of us would want to repeat those earlier years. ADDulthood has its ups and downs, but the downs don't compare to those of childhood. When your child is diagnosed you can't escape painfully revisiting your own past. And you think, "It doesn't seem fair that I have to do this again." Or even more than that, that they have to go through the same thing.

A Way Around It—Try to separate your experiences from those of your child (or children). He or she is unique, in spite of your common problem of ADD. On the positive side, his or her experience does not have to be as difficult as yours was, especially because we have more knowledge about ADD now, and there is more help out there. And be thankful that your child has a parent who can empathize with his or her problems.

"When spiderwebs unite, they can tie up a lion."
—*Ethiopian proverb*

We feel very optimistic about the prospects for adults with ADD in the next few years. Since the late 1980s, when recognition that ADD continues into adulthood began to seep into the public consciousness, we have been fighting an uphill battle to get help for ourselves. We have fought with professionals who denied us treatment because they were not knowledgeable about ADD. We have fought with insurance companies who denied payment for the disorder. And we have fought legal battles for accommodations at work and in school.

But at first we were only a handful of people, a few who got the message before information about ADD became major news. Now we are many. The news stories and talk shows have helped, the positive ones lifting our spirits and enlightening those who have experienced ADD only from the outside. And the negative comments have spurred us on to greater efforts to counter the false images. As a group, we now have efficient ways to organize and communicate with each other. The Internet, for example, is a powerful tool that we are using to help each other and build a power base for change—not only for ourselves, but for our children as well.

A Way Around It—Give your spirit a boost of empowerment by becoming active in the fight to help yourself and your ADD brothers and sisters. You don't have to make it a career or spend all your free time doing it. Simply speak up when the opportunity presents itself, and write letters to policy makers when an issue comes to your attention. But do something, for now and for the future.

"I can't help detesting my relations. I suppose it comes from the fact that none of us can stand other people having the same faults as ourselves."

—*Oscar Wilde*

With ADD being a genetic disorder, it is almost impossible to escape seeing some of our worst ADD traits mirrored in our relatives. This is probably why so many of us flee the family homestead as soon as possible, and why it is so hard to find the time to get back for visits. Of course, there are other reasons for this behavior, such as the better availability of jobs or the wish to live in a different climate. We do live in a highly mobile society. But isn't a part of you sighing with relief because your family of origin lives in another state? Or do you find yourself wishing that they did? Especially if they don't own up to their ADD or do anything to modify themselves and their actions. And who can blame us? We have worked so hard on ourselves since diagnosis that it is painful to be confronted with the unadorned ADD of close relatives. They are what we used to be, and still are when we don't watch ourselves. And we have to struggle with a strong urge to convert Mom or Dad or Grandpa to our new understanding and worldview. But they usually don't want to change. In fact, they resist any suggestion that they might have this thing that they don't really believe in anyway.

A Way Around It—Don't feel guilty about keeping your distance from your family of origin. Until you can accept them as they are, resisting the urge to preach about ADD, staying away will do all of you a favor. Later, when you have gone further in your recovery, you will find your visits easier, whether they change or not. And when they see the difference in you, they will be more likely to investigate this ADD thing.

"I know the answer! The answer lies within the heart of all mankind! The answer is twelve? I think I'm in the wrong building."

—*Charles Schulz*

We really do know the answer much of the time. Or at least some part of the answer. But that impulse to impress people, to show them that we really aren't so dumb, can trip us up. Anxious for a chance to shine, if only for a brief moment, up shoots our hand, before we fully process the question or formulate the answer. Sometimes we get away with it, and that lucky fluke lures us to try the same tactic next time. Usually, though, we end up with the proverbial egg on our faces, stumbling and stuttering out a half-baked reply.

A Way Around It—Take the time to listen and reflect before responding. Your patience will be rewarded. After all, you want people to note and remember the times you are on target, rather than those endless rounds of shooting practice.

"A friend knows how to allow for mere quantity in your talk, and only replies to quality."

—*Anonymous*

Why does it seem as if your friends never listen to you? You get halfway through an anecdote or story, and your audience turns a deaf ear. A bosom buddy is supposed to stay riveted to the spot, while you pour out all the fascinating details of your life, right? Like the complete history of your medical problems in gory detail. Or an endless recitation of the plot of the movie you saw last night. Why not? *You* think this stuff is utterly fascinating. So you think that maybe it's your friend's fault. He or she should do something about their ADD. And then you would finally have an attentive listener for your verbal productions.

A Way Around It—Is it ADD or just a natural human response to a barrage of words? ADD or not, the bottom line is that you can't change your friends. Instead, you can use their nonverbal cues as guidelines for working on yourself. When you lose their attention, it is time to stop, change the subject, or ask your friend about their life.

"There is nothing permanent except change."

—*Heraclitus*

It's rather funny, actually. So much is unpredictable. About the only thing we can predict with certainty is that things will keep changing!

Change is always scary. Even positive changes cause stress, because change causes a disruption in daily life. It requires the dismantling and subsequent rebuilding of long-held practices, beliefs, and operating systems. And it requires a readjustment in the relationships with significant others, some of whom may not be aware of your changes.

Think about what happens in a marriage when one partner is diagnosed and treated for ADD. The whole equation changes dramatically. Initially, both partners may find themselves feeling as if they are on their second honeymoon. This often doesn't last, however, because . . . change is inevitable. First, old baggage has a way of getting recycled because memories don't magically disappear. Second, the newly diagnosed spouse isn't the same person he or she used to be. And third, the non-ADDer isn't sure who this new person is: The spouse is clearly not the same person he or she married years earlier. All these changes conspire to upset the apple cart, as they say.

A Way Around It—Don't get discouraged if personal changes seem for a time to make things worse. Long-standing relationships take a long time to undergo change as partners readjust expectations and ways of mutually responding. Just keep communication channels open, seeking help from a marriage counselor, if necessary, to help the two of you find a new definition for your changed relationship.

"I like long walks, especially when they are taken by people who annoy me."

—*Fred Allen*

It's amazing how long an hour can feel when it's spent in the company of an in-law complaining of arthritis or a child asking for the umpteenth time, "But, why?" And how about those warm, wonderful times when the extended family comes together for holiday festivities: the nieces and nephews fighting over the video machine; the new baby screaming with colic; the mother-in-law *tsk*ing over unironed table linens. Your brain screams for relief from the onslaught of overstimulation. And, as if he can read your mind, Uncle Harry provides an answer to prayer by suggesting that everyone bundle up and go outside to have a snowball fight. Phew!

The nature of our disorder is such that it doesn't take much to send us into a frantic state, feeling as if we are being squeezed inside a ball of rubber bands. This experience of continual conflict isn't limited to the home front. At work you find yourself enduring colleagues who interrupt with uninvited visits to your desk and your officemate who shares, ad nauseam, the details of the upcoming company banquet he is organizing. You seethe, secretly wishing you could simply affix a large piece of masking tape to each respective mouth or erect a wall of cement between you and the offending parties.

A Way Around It—It's essential that you have space in which to think, work, and just be. It's impossible to exist as if you were the only person on the planet, but you can and should establish well-thought-out personal boundaries, clearly communicating them to those with whom you live and work. Initial boundary setting will involve negotiation and compromise. After the rules have been determined, however, be ruthless about sticking to your guns.

"What do you mean we don't communicate? Just yesterday I faxed you a reply to the recorded message you left on my answering machine."

—*Anonymous*

It's become difficult these days to use the old excuse that *it must have gotten lost in the mail.* Lost in cyberspace is more like it. Although you still can't fax your mortgage payment to the bank, you can use electronic banking to get the job done quickly and efficiently. You can design an anniversary card with your computer software, e-mailing it to your spouse just in the nick of time. Not to worry, your computer's personal information manager will prompt you with a preset alarm when the big day has arrived.

Assuming that you've figured out how to operate successfully the varied wonders of modern electronic wizardry, your response time in many situations can be dramatically decreased and the quality of your responses improved. Rather than impulsively saying something to your boss that you wish a super-duper word vacuum could instantly suck back in, you have time to write a measured response. Just be careful about reducing all communication to the electronic variety—successful performance on the job depends on more than robotic actions. Success in the workplace, as in every other arena of your life, depends on developing satisfactory interpersonal relationships. As useful as fax and answering machines and computers are, they don't do much for team brainstorming sessions . . . and they make lousy business lunch partners!

A Way Around It—These days, it's critical that you acquire some basic skills of modern telecommunication. Take advantage of whatever in-house training and hands-on workshops your company offers or sponsors. If you aren't computer savvy, it's a good idea to do some practice runs e-mailing messages to yourself or a friend. And don't *ever* forget that e-mail messages are *not* private, so be careful about that note to your colleague in which you characterize your officemate as a frustrated eunuch! Finally, remember that all the fancy electronic gadgets in the world will never replace good old-fashioned face-to-face communication.

"The mind is like a TV set—when it goes blank, it's a good idea to turn off the sound."

—Anonymous

I love to talk. About anything and everything. It's not that I love the sound of my own voice. It's just that talking serves as a safety valve, releasing the pressure cooker my brain becomes when thoughts and ideas start ricocheting around. Even when I've emptied my mind of the pressing thoughts and feelings, my mouth somehow doesn't get the message and keeps moving of its own volition!

I'm sure that if I don't keep expressing myself—even after I've said everything that could possibly be considered worth saying—I'll explode. Of course I won't literally come apart if I don't pour my heart out to the nearest sentient being, but it sure feels like that sometimes.

This need to get everything out of my mind and off my chest results in pressured speech that often tortures my listeners. Not only don't they have a prayer of contributing their thoughts, they also have to attempt to follow the convoluted path my talking takes after I've been at it awhile!

There's nothing wrong with venting now and then, assuming your listener doesn't mind being the sounding board. This variety of talking, however, isn't conducive to genuine and effective communication, because that requires an interchange of information—talking . . . and listening. In the absence of real back-and-forth dialogue, your speech becomes a monologue and your words just noise, like the static on your TV set at 4 A.M., when no signals are broadcast.

A Way Around It—When you feel the need to talk for the sake of talking, let the other person know that that's what you're doing. And try periodically checking to be sure your listener hasn't fallen asleep or has smoke emitting from his ears, frustrated to the max—ask, "Is my talking making you crazy?" And here's another thought. Talking to oneself might be thought crazy, but it's really not such a bad idea. If this is your preferred channel for thinking and processing information, it can be a valuable way to clean house, so to speak, before you start talking to somebody else.

—P. R.

"We never talked, my family. We communicated by putting Ann Landers articles on the refrigerator."
—*Judy Gold*

Some families use a message board, the answering machine, or Post-it notes on the bathroom mirror. An urgent message taped to the toilet seat in such a way that you can't take a pee unless you deal with the note is one way to grab the erratic attention of ADD family members. All of these methods of communication have their uses, but they also have fatal flaws. When you have ADD, it is all too easy to walk right by the message board or answering machine without noticing that a stack of important messages awaits. Unless the Post-its cover the entire mirror, it is possible to shave or put your face on without giving them a passing thought. Not to mention that it seems pointless even to have a family when you never meet and communicate face-to-face.

A Way Around It—Work toward honest and direct communication with loved ones. Be aware, however, that avoidance is the path of least resistance. Expect some backsliding along the road to better communication.

6

Work, Work, Work, Work . . .

What do you mean we don't have recess?
&$(@$#!

Oh, the cold, hard reality of adult life, when the milk and cookie breaks disappear, or are much too far apart for our tastes. Eight hours is an ungodly length of time to be chained to a computer, a desk, or a repetitive task. And some of us are not even lucky enough to have a circumscribed end to our days. It is kind of insulting and demeaning to have to punch a clock, but at least you get to go home at the proper time, or be paid overtime for your extra work. Those poor salaried workers don't know where the work ends and the rest of life begins, because unfinished work goes home with them. In today's "lean and mean" environment the work never seems to be finished anyway, so how can you win? Owning your own business is no panacea, either, because then the twenty-four-hour buck passes to you.

Please, please, please don't let these realities move you to give up in despair, however. There are ways to make the world of work more bearable and sometimes even rewarding. As ADDers, we have a set of unique problems to wrestle with in the workplace, in addition to the ones that everyone else has. But we also bring our special gifts to the office, or other workplace. We are often full of energy, enthusiasm, and novel ideas. Since we think and view the world in an unconventional fashion, we are more likely to see beyond the old, tired ways of doing things and discover a fresh solution to knotty problems.

Of course, there is a hitch. It's a variation on the "square peg in a round hole" problem.

ADDults often have a history written in many short-term jobs, often of less than a year in length. We may frequently move to the next job or challenge because our work has become dull, uninteresting, or limiting in some way. In addition, we live in constant fear that our employers will discover we have ADD, so we literally plan when we need to leave to avoid facing another put-down or failure because of our disability.

Succeeding in the workplace requires not only creativity and "smarts," which we ADDers often have in ample amounts, but also the ability to listen, monitor social cues and body language, and figure out what our bosses are really asking us to do. While our work tasks may be less profound than we would like, they are still important to those we work for. If we want to keep our jobs, we must accept what it is we are being paid to do. Agreeing to do the task we were hired to complete is the first step to being successful in the workplace, but for ADDers it's only the first step. Visualizing, working for, and creating for ourselves the job we really want is the goal.

"A committee is a thing which takes a week to do what
  one good man can do in an hour."
                                              —*Elbert Hubbard*

We don't know how many of you have had to endure the
torture of working on a committee, but based on our experience, we don't recommend it. The ADDers we know
tend to be people of action. We want to brainstorm a solution and then get on with the work of actually solving the
problem. In contrast, committees tend to beat a problem
to death by overanalyzing it until it is too late to do anything about it. They seem to require a strange kind of attitude from their members, which is the willingness to spend
a long time talking about a problem without fixing it.

   Of course, there are some advantages to the committee
way of doing business. For one thing, you have a whole
group to pass the buck around to, if things go wrong. And
sometimes it's nice to bask in the false security you get
when the committee actually gets around to laying out
some kind of plan. Except that you know from past experience the plan is likely to change, or be trashed altogether.
In theory, committees have the advantage of bringing
more than one set of abilities to the problem-solving table.
In reality, this benefit is an asset only when the members
can put aside their differences in order to work together.

A Way Around It—Exercise caution when it comes to
signing up for committee work. A little of it goes a long
way for most of us. If you find yourself stuck on one of the
darn things, consider it a lesson in patience and fortitude.
On the other hand, don't rule out the option of working
with a partner, or in a very small, informal group. Two
heads can be better than one, if we are willing to put some
effort into the working relationships.

"Work is the greatest thing in the world, so we should always save some of it for tomorrow."

—*Don Herold*

We don't know if we agree about its being the greatest thing since sliced bread, but we do know that work is never really finished. There is always something more to do. For ADDults, learning how to spread a project over days, weeks, or months does not come easily. We sweat over the small details and worry about the ones that have inevitably slipped our minds. We also fear that if we don't get it all done *right now*, we will lose our momentum.

When we are no longer inspired or excited, we want to drop a project like a hot potato. We are amazed at people who can work on a project until a designated quitting time and then stop, resuming the next day where they left off. Each of us tries to set our work hours, but we find that putting the project to bed for the night is always a struggle. We always fear that if we don't keep working until a job is done, we will never finish it.

A Way Around It—A good way to work through this issue is to practice multitasking, to have several projects going at the same time. It helps you avoid becoming too obsessed with a particular project, and it can keep the boredom at bay. To be successful at this, however, you need to use an organized system to keep the jobs moving along and to avoid mixing them up in your head. Break up each project into smaller pieces with deadlines assigned to each task. Post your task and deadline list in a prominent place. Also, make sure that each project has its own folder or file.

"I not only use all the brains I have, but all I can borrow."
—*Woodrow Wilson*

I love it every time I read about an achiever who is a fan of teamwork, a big shot who is humble enough to admit to the truth. The truth is that no one makes it on their own. All the great accomplishments in history came about through the efforts of many, even if they weren't recognized for their contribution. Life is too complicated for one person to figure out singlehandedly.

As an ADD youth, I never had the chance to learn much about teamwork. I was always the one the other kids didn't want on their team, because I could not stay focused and got into trouble all the time. I was the one who got into fights and went to the principal's office two or three times a week. As an adult, the situation is different. I have better self-control than I did when I was a child. And I have learned that when I work with other people, sharing ideas, effort, and recognition, the results are better than anything I could do alone.

A Way Around It—Use all the people resources you can gather when you have a project to do. Work at establishing and maintaining rapport with your collaborators. The mutual support, fresh ideas, and different points of view are worth the work involved in a partnership.

—D. S. L.

"I yield to no one in my admiration for the office as a social centre, but it's no place actually to get any work done."
—*Katherine Whitehorn*

What a relief to realize that one is not alone with this particular problem. I used to blame myself when I never seemed to reach my daily workload goals. It was my distractibility, I thought, and a lack of discipline. Now, when I look back at those pre-ADD awareness days, I realize that it was far more complicated than that.

Sure, the ADD interfered with getting started and staying on track, but my internal difficulties were only part of the struggle. Although I worked hard at putting that old nose to the grindstone, just as soon as I got settled and concentrated on a task, some unavoidable distraction would present itself. The boss would call a mandatory meeting, a coworker would come to me with a personal problem, or the office would throw a good-bye party for someone.

I could usually see the purpose in stopping for the last two things, but it seemed to me that the meetings were held largely because the boss was tired of sitting alone in her office, wrestling with her own restlessness. I quickly learned that for me to ignore any of these "social" requests would have been a major mistake, because task completion is only one part of a job description.

A Way Around It—Work on improving your concentration and focus, but try not to become obsessed with this as the total picture. Even if you're perfectly disciplined, your day will still be interrupted by other needs and priorities. For instance, the relationships with your coworkers are at least as important as the tasks, especially when you need to work as a team.

—K. K.

"I don't know how it is that you start working at something that you don't like, and before you know it you're an old man."

—Herman Mankiewicz

This is a sad but true scenario for many of us. We have these flashes of brilliance, multiple gifts, and creative talents. But we lack the focus to make them into a coherent whole, to decide what we want to be when we grow up. Some of us leave our options open on a permanent basis, refusing to do anything that requires us to choose or make a commitment. Then we may think that we are "free."

But free to do what? We may not have the same dull nine-to-five job year after year, but anything truly fulfilling requires a degree of commitment. Another path many of us choose is to opt for a vocation that is not the best fit but that seems tolerable, at least. It may seem to offer security or structure. Over the years, however, that vocation is more and more loathsome. It is too deadly boring, or it saps our energy without giving any of it back.

A Way Around It—If you hate what you are doing, it is not too late to change it. Discover your true profession and pursue it. You don't have to make the change overnight. In fact, we specifically recommend that you *don't*. Take your time and do some research before you take any action. If you neglect to do your homework, you could end up spending your time and money training for something that is even worse than the job you presently hold. In the end, if you have to take a cut in pay or status, the benefits are preferable to letting your soul shrivel and die.

"Meds can move mountains in the mind; but, shovel in hand, I still have to show up for work every day."

—*Joe O'Connor*

It is so hard to get back to work after the mind-blowing experience of a good response to medication. Your head is clear—for the first time in your life—and you can see a panorama of all the possibilities in yourself and your life. But it takes so long to actually make any of those promises real. And there is so much gritty work to be done along the way, both at your job and in your ADD recovery.

You find that the office is even more boring than before, and worse, that you've lost all patience with yourself, with your personal progress. So it is natural to get discouraged, or even downright despondent from time to time. How do you learn to stay on the farm, so to speak, when you have seen those bright city lights?

A Way Around It—Those visions of possibility are real and attainable, but gratification will certainly not be immediate. In the meantime, believe in yourself and keep your vision of a better life in your mind's eye. It will fortify you as you do the hard work needed to realize your goals.

"The brain is a wonderful organ; it starts working the moment you get up in the morning and does not stop until you get to the office."

—*Robert Frost*

Some brains start working at the first buzz of the alarm clock. Ours are likely to wait until a more civilized hour. Let's say noon. Some days, it may seem as if they never quite get into the working mode at all. They always seem to need an oil change or a tune-up or something.

Many ADDers confess that their bodies go through the routines of getting ready for work, and perform the morning tasks at the office, but that their minds are not fully engaged. At those times, we are like the walking dead, and we pray nothing happens that would require us actually to think. It's as if we're on autopilot, hoping everyone else thinks we're flying the plane.

A Way Around It—Perhaps you can rearrange things a little in your life so that you do most of the work when your brain is at its peak. After all, our rhythms are not those of everyone else. Look into self-employment opportunities. If that's just not possible, or you don't yet have the self-discipline to work on your own, perhaps you can find a job with flexible hours.

"If you hate your job, either change your job or change your attitude about the job. One or the other."
—*John-Roger*

We can imagine the reaction of our ADD readers to this quote. When you hear such words, your first reaction may be to stiffen defensively. "What do you mean change my job? I'm stuck with this rotten job because I have to make a living! I can't change my boss, the working conditions, or my coworkers. So how can I manage an attitude transplant?"

Well, it won't be easy, but the alternative is much worse. It is true that you can't change the behavior of other people. It is also true that an immediate job or career change may be impractical. You can, however, take steps and make plans to find a better work situation in the future. In the meantime, it is important to find a way to live with the job you have. The negative feelings you have toward the job will only impact negatively on your mental and physical health.

A Way Around It—Do something, however small, toward making that future job change a reality. Make a list of possibilities and do some research on careers or opportunities that intrigue you. Until you are able to actualize your plans, consider modifying the psychological investment you have in your current job. Have you placed this job at the center of your life? If so, it may help if you put more of your mental energy elsewhere, into relationships or outside activities. Remember, your job is not all that you are.

"Hard work never killed anybody, but why take a chance?"
—*Charlie McCarthy*

Here's a handy rebuttal for those snide comments directed at our "laziness." Of course we are not truly lazy (or stupid, or crazy). It just takes us longer to get started on a project, or to crank up into gear and start the workday. Furthermore, when we finally manage to get in the working mode, we can astonish ourselves and coworkers with the results of our efforts.

"They" wonder how on earth that marvelous presentation, piece of advertising copy, or proposal emerged from all the time we spent doodling and noodling around. What "they" don't understand is that the apparently aimless activity we engage in before we actually produce anything is not as purposeless as it seems. We were actually thinking and planning the whole time, if a bit chaotically. But who ever said that the creative process was meant to be orderly?

A Way Around It—Give your unique working style the respect it deserves. If you find that scribbling, pacing the room, staring into space, or making endless trips on the elevator helps you get your thoughts into workable order, follow your instincts and tune out the disapproving comments. As long as you aren't interfering with someone else's time or space, your methods are nobody's business but your own.

"Don't tell me no!"

—*Robert J. Ramundo*

This quote is a mantra contributed by my husband. Even as a toddler, he was recognizable as a typical "type A" personality. In elementary school, he practiced his future profession as a businessman by lending money to family and friends at healthy interest rates. A five-dollar loan today was payable at six dollars one week later. Not a huge amount of money—unless you are ten years old. I'm sure Donald Trump would be green with envy. Wouldn't he love to earn a 20 percent return on his investment in a week's time!

Rob is an ADDer with a driving force to succeed sitting at the core of his very soul. It is not about money, really, loan-sharking activities notwithstanding! For Rob, business is an exciting game, a game that is even juicier when the deck is stacked against him. While he admits that his response to the word *no* is sometimes unprintable, much of the time the challenge inspires an extra twinkle in his eye and a renewed commitment to face down the obstacles.

A Way Around It—As ADDers, we have often been reprimanded for having a bad attitude, especially toward authority. But is it the attitude that is at fault, or just the presentation? Obscenities and hostility are certainly not acceptable responses when you meet with resistance, but just giving up or giving in is not the answer either. If you truly believe in your idea or project, go for it, but do spend some time considering how you can best approach the person who is saying, "It can't be done."

—P. R.

"Most of us are umpires at heart: we like to call balls and strikes on somebody else."

—*Leo Aikman*

Isn't that the truth? Lunch with a friend from the office is a great arena for playing umpire. His voice joins yours in an ever growing diatribe against the newest member of the company whose inexperience and bumbling is screwing up the current project your team is working on. And, hey, that V.P. whose slave-driving is leading to a mutiny in the ranks, he's a real piece of work, isn't he? Heck, if it wasn't for the interference of these people, your job would be a breeze, right? Reality-check time. As an old axiom says, When you point your finger at that coworker, three fingers are pointing back at you! It seems the nature of the human beast is to criticize other people, probably in part as a defense against having to give a long, hard look at oneself. Discovering that we are lacking in some way isn't a discovery we want to make.

A Way Around It—Don't beat yourself up for the times you find yourself playing umpire. It certainly can protect you from being overly self-critical. But the strategy back-fires when your energy and efforts are only focused on negativity. When you start thinking or talking about the shortcomings of your boss, balance these criticisms with some positive statements. Can't think of any? Then try following the age-old axiom: "If you can't think of anything nice to say, don't say anything at all!"

"Have I reached the person to whom I am speaking?"
—*Lily Tomlin as "Ernestine"*

Many of us have laughed at the antics of Lily Tomlin's Ernestine, the telephone operator. We laugh in recognition, having experienced the frustration of miscommunication. Now, if you are the parent of either a toddler or an adolescent, you may feel like giving up on ever "reaching the person to whom you are speaking." Two-year-olds and sixteen-year-olds seem to share the inability to hear anything you say!

Parent-child miscommunication aside, misunderstandings often occur because we fail to consider the critical role of body language in conveying messages. In fact, experts say that words make up less than 20 percent of communication. The largest part of the message is conveyed through body language, the nonverbal cues.

Keeping this in mind is especially important in the workplace, where you have to respond to frequent "on-the-fly" comments and directives. Your boss tells you to do something, finishing the dialogue with, "Let me know if I can help you?" If you don't pay attention to her nonverbal cue—looking at her watch as she quickly moves away from you—you might launch into a lengthy reply. Her body language should alert you to her impatience and unwillingness to converse with you at the moment.

The quality of your communication with others depends on your awareness of the role body language plays in these interchanges. What you see provides information that can be more valuable than that of the spoken words. And of course the same applies to the body language you use. Remember that your visual cues convey unspoken words to your listener.

A Way Around It—If you aren't getting what you need and want from others, you may be sending the wrong body messages. Work at presenting yourself as a confident person. Use these basic "body-talk" tips of Germaine Knapp, founder of a Rochester, New York, communications consulting firm: Sit or stand erect; lean slightly forward; maintain eye contact; unfold your arms and legs; look open, pleasant, and positive; nod your head occasionally and say "yes" to emphasize agreement; sit at the head of the table or stand while others are seated to show command.

"The only thing more overrated than natural childbirth is the joy of owning your own business."

—*Anonymous*

I can add a loud "Amen" to this sentiment, having endured fourteen excruciatingly painful and joyless hours of labor, and twenty-five-plus years of owning several businesses with my husband. The latter experience has been only slightly less painful and marginally more joyful than those hours spent giving birth!

Don't get me wrong: The entrepreneurial bent of many ADDers can make owning your own business an enticing possibility. Doing it your way can allow you to make better use of talents that might otherwise go unused and unrecognized when you try to fit your ADD quirks into someone else's business organization.

If you have never found a satisfying work environment within corporate America and have a particular, marketable skill, setting off on your own can be the catalyst you need to attain personal satisfaction and financial success. Launching your own business, however, is not an endeavor for the faint of heart. Expect a long gestation period, lots of aches and pains along the way, and deliveries way behind schedule!

A Way Around It—Don't let me scare you into backing away from your entrepreneurial dreams! I merely want to inject a note of caution for your consideration as you make plans and choices. Take it from one whose wisdom was earned the hard way. Resist the temptation to jump into a business start-up with nothing but ideas and enthusiasm. Do your homework obsessively, making sure you have adequate financial resources and a detailed business plan before that production line starts running.

—P. R.

7

Organizing Time and Space

They say that time is a gift to be treasured. That's fine for poets and philosophers, but talk about rose-colored glasses—get real! If time is a gift, it appears to many of us ADDers that it's been given by a sadist, intent on torturing us for some terrible thing we've done. What a rotten thing to do—giving us a gift that should have been recalled for defects in manufacturing, because it doesn't work worth a damn. Can't we just exchange it or, better yet, receive a full refund?

It's no wonder we have a love-hate relationship with time. It's a tick-tock terror that is two-faced and as temperamental as we are! At times, it flies . . . at times it seems to stand still. It's a tease and a lousy team player. It's like this: It's the critical play of the game. . . . We look around for some time and it's nowhere to be found. . . . Time just plain ran out! So, with no remaining time-outs on the clock, we're up against the wall—it's deadline time. And, of course we don't have any spare time on our hands (or anywhere else for that matter!), so we set out to buy some more—ah, yes, if only we could just pick some up at the grocery story along with milk and orange juice! Since we can't do that, we borrow it from somewhere in our already overly busy schedules, discovering that what we've really done is stolen it, unable to "pay it back"!

We know we're in trouble when a stranger casually asks, "Do you have the time?" and we have to fight the urge to snarl back, "What are you, crazy or something? If I had any time, do you think I'd be this frantic and wild-eyed, gasping for air as I race down the sidewalk pushing people aside? And even if I had the time, do you think I'd share even one millisecond of it with a complete stranger?"

Humor aside, organizing our lives is a Herculean task for many of us. If managing time were simply a matter of being able to "tell time"—a skill we learned when we were five or six years old—there wouldn't be a problem. Unfortunately, try as we might to *tell time*, it never seems to listen! As Irishman Finley Peter Dunne said in 1910 in "Things Spiritual," *Mr. Dooley Says*, "Scales and clocks ar-re not to be thrusted to decide anything that's worth deciding. Who tells time be a clock? Ivry hour is th' same to a clock an' ivry hour is diff'rent to me. Wan long, wan short." Isn't that the truth?

Although we often personalize time, ascribing to it qualities of a living, breathing tyrant, it is, of course, merely a concept, a framework within which we structure the events of our daily lives. Within the dimension of time we organize the sequencing of spatial events against a backdrop of the duration of time itself, which comes in three varieties—*my time, their time,* and *shared time.* "My time" is the internal time needed to learn something or to enjoy personal satisfaction that operates within individual, biological rhythms—our innate, twenty-four-hour circadian cycles of peak and nonpeak performance times. This is distinct from "their time," the external time within which we are expected to respond to the pressure to perform a task, do it, and then be judged according to the speed and quality of our performance. Finally, there is "shared time," the merging of one's personal time rhythms with those of others within the larger context of "real time," as it were.

The struggle for time is the basis for the daily dilemmas we human beings face as we attempt to organize our activities to fit within this larger perspective of time. How long does it take to do something? How do I find the time to do both the things I must do and those that I want to do? And then, what happens when my time conflicts with yours, for example when I have to wait for you to do something before I can do what I need to do, and vice versa? Stress is typically the fallout from these conflicts. Our response is typically to consult assorted self-help books looking for time-saving tips, a strategy that nearly always backfires. It backfires because of the Law of Time: To-do lists always expand to fit whatever time is available. Accepting this reality is the place to start if we are to gain some control over our lives.

Consider the complexity of this concept we call organization, a process that includes the components of attention, memory, and learning. The effective ordering of the events of our lives within the multidimensional aspects of my time, their time, and shared time(s) requires attention to detail and the ability to plan ahead, sorting and filing all these elements into an external framework, as well as having an adequate memory to remember the assorted details. Since so many of us have varying degrees of weaknesses in these skills, it's not surprising that *dis*-order often becomes a way of life. But we don't have to feel out of control all the time, because despite the problems inherent to our ADD, each of us can become self-empowered through personal choice. We can decide to do things differently. Your decision to act or *not to act* on this choice largely determines how successful you will be at organizing your life, and the degree of stress—or peace—you will experience.

On the following pages, we will explore the havoc disorganization wreaks and suggest ways to minimize its effects. You will read some *tried and true* strategies for making better use of your time and for organizing your belongings, and also some ideas for you to think about regarding the personal choices you make in your daily life. These "think-abouts" aren't specific tips as much as they are food for your personal introspective thought. We hope they will provide a somewhat different perspective about time and stuff management, one that focuses on quality rather than quantity—how to enjoy personal peace and order through simplicity.

"I hate housework. You make the beds, wash the dishes, etc. And six months later you have to start the whole thing over again."

—*Joan Rivers*

Unless it is an annual event, as it is for some of us. We beat ourselves up over the silliest things. Okay, so we can see the point of washing the dishes at least weekly, because they smell bad if you don't. Plus you run out of plates after a while. But what's wrong with paper plates? We know, it's the environment, stupid!

However, there is no conclusive evidence that using china or stoneware plates is better for the environment anyhow. What about the water, electricity, and detergent it takes to get them clean? And is it really essential that we make our beds? It is nice once in a while to get into a freshly made bed, but it really doesn't have to be a daily event. *Make thy bed* was not one of the dictates handed down to Moses by God, as far as we can recollect.

A Way Around It—Give yourself permission to cut whatever housekeeping corners you need to in order to grab some free time and space for yourself. No one ever lay on their deathbed wishing they had spent more time doing housework.

"The only way of catching a train I ever discovered is to miss the train before."

—*G. K. Chesterton*

This is a good metaphor for a life spent playing catch-up in a number of realms. A groggy, sleepy brain needs a wake-up call well in advance of actually attempting to do anything. An alarm clock helps, as do the various morning rituals you do as you slowly come to. But nothing works quite like the shot of adrenaline you get from a minor fright or a close call.

Now, missing a train is not a big deal in the total scheme of things. Still, you can get a minor rush from the process and challenge of trying to beat the clock. And when you do miss that first train anyway, your mind is more alert and you have plenty of time to dawdle over breakfast as you wait for the next one. Perhaps the same dynamic applies when it comes to relationships and jobs. We hope so. It would be nice to find out that all those false starts, all the preparedness and excitement, have had a purpose after all. They served as practice, getting you ready, fit, and sassy for when your special train, the one you're supposed to get on, comes along.

A Way Around It—Do make plans, preparing as much as you can in advance and attempting to keep to some kind of a schedule. But be prepared for false starts and detours. You'll be surprised at how well you can master the art of rushing to wait and to use it to your advantage. As a bonus, you'll learn a little patience, too.

"Punctuality is something that, if you have it, there's often no one around to share it with you."

—*Anonymous*

And it is vastly overrated. We know this, because we have spent much of our adult lives trying to master time management skills. When we were successful, our punctuality became a point of self-righteousness used as a weapon to clobber the habitually late. Don't get us wrong, it is inconsiderate to keep people waiting for long stretches of time and to do it regularly. But everyone gets stuck in traffic or delayed by their children now and then.

In the long run, a few minutes waiting for someone else or occasional tardiness on your own part is nothing to fuss and fume about. Chronic lateness is another story. If you are on the receiving end, don't expect that you can force, cajole, or reason the other person out of this behavior. You can let them know how it affects you, and you can ultimately stop making plans with a person who doesn't show up on time. But the only behavior you can really change is your own.

A Way Around It—Try to be reasonably punctual most of the time, in consideration of others. But do exercise patience with others in this regard, keeping in mind the times and reasons you've been late. However, don't let this equation become too unbalanced. If a friend is consistently late, talk about it. Don't accuse, but explain how it makes you feel when you are kept waiting. If you are the habitually tardy one, examine your own behavior with the goal of making some changes. For specific advice on time management techniques, read chapter 13 in *You Mean I'm Not Lazy, Stupid or Crazy?!*

"I don't know how it happens. My car just drives itself to Neiman-Marcus."

—*Victoria Principal*

The same thing has happened to me, but instead of Neiman-Marcus, I find myself in the parking lot of Value City. I never intended to go there. I've made a vow to cut back on the spending, and anyway, I'm supposed to be at my desk, writing, or cleaning my house or something. I confess, however, that the urge for forward motion, especially when faced with difficult or boring tasks, is irresistible.

In a trance, I am propelled forward into my vehicle before I can register a protest. In all honesty, though, I wouldn't object too much or too loudly anyway. Once inside the store, I wander around in a daze, searching for the retail equivalent of the Holy Grail. Sometimes I find it, the bargain of the century. But it usually isn't what I thought I was looking for when I went in the store. Much of the time, the shopping trip ends up as an exercise in confusion and frustration.

A Way Around It—It isn't easy to break this particular way of killing time or procrastinating. It may help to schedule regular shopping expeditions with a list and budget in hand. And when faced with odious tasks, try to find a less expensive and time-consuming distraction, such as taking a walk. In short, take a break but don't take forever.

—K. K.

"I've found a great way to start the day—I go straight back to bed!"

—*Anonymous*

Left to our own devices, this is exactly what a lot of us would do. When we hold jobs or responsibilities requiring us to get up and out in the morning, we don't have to wrestle with this problem in quite the same way as the unemployed and self-employed. It is no fun to drag ourselves out of bed on a gray morning when we look and feel like Medusa's twin. But at least the problem of choosing a direction for the day is solved.

Fear can be highly motivating! We are afraid of what the boss will do or say, and we anticipate how resentful our co-workers will be when they have to take up the slack. Reluctantly, we drag ourselves out of that bed, deciding that facing the day is the lesser evil. The immediate consequences of pulling those covers back over our heads stare us right in the face. It is much harder when we work on our own. We will eventually have to pay the piper in terms of generating income, but the day of reckoning is usually further off.

A *Way Around It*—Know thyself when it comes to selecting an occupation and lifestyle. If you have great difficulty structuring your time and getting started, postpone that dream of self-employment until you have learned how to set up and follow a routine. Consult an ADD coach if you have problems doing this on your own. They specialize in helping ADDers with structure and time management.

"I try to order my belongings, but they never listen to me."
—*Don Lambert*

It's not fair! Nobody listens to us at home or at the office. We all need someone or something to boss around, to be in charge of. But nobody wants to take the subordinate role. Even the cat and dog need remedial obedience school training, and they are surly, uncooperative students. At least we ought to be able to control and take charge of our stuff, our own personal possessions, right? With ADD, though, even the stuff of life is rebellious. It simply refuses to conform to the systems and rules we try to impose.

A Way Around It—Perhaps it's the rules and the systems that are at fault. Organizational plans with too much rigid control and order are doomed to failure, mainly because life is never that orderly. You do need a game plan or plans for organizing your things, but be prepared to change them as your needs change.

"I don't think I've used a hanger in my entire life. I have always enjoyed living in my own debris."

—*Steven Spielberg*

The $64,000 question is whether disorder is a lifestyle choice or a monster over which we have no control. It is not, as some people think, just a matter of some central defect in the brain's organizational skill center. There is no such place, because the brain is much more complicated and mysterious than that. So where does the "mess monster" come from?

It may seem like a monster, but it is really just a natural tendency that has gotten out of hand. If you and your family don't mind living in a lot of clutter, and if you can find your stuff when you need it, it's not a problem. On the other hand, if the litter in your life constantly gets in your way, it's time to do something about it. Perfect order, however, is never the goal. Striving for it puts us at risk for another problem, obsessive-compulsive behaviors. So, how does one decide how much disorder to tolerate, and on what basis?

A Way Around It—Examine your motives for attacking your messes or for letting them slide. Most people swing back and forth to some degree. If you find that you are largely driven by shame or defiance, you are not making a conscious choice about the excess or lack of tidiness in your life. If you can't seem to reach a healthy balance in the area of clutter control, you may need to consult a good therapist for help with the underlying psychological issues.

"Looking back, my life seems like one long obstacle race, with me as its chief obstacle."

—Jack Paar

We complain about all the interruptions at home and at work, and often think that we would get along just fine if only "others" would just leave us alone. That is only part of the story, however. Picture this: You finally have some time to yourself at home, when your spouse and kids take that out-of-town trip. It's peaceful and quiet, because you have unplugged the phone and disabled the doorbell.

And there you sit, restless and fidgeting at your desk, unable to write a word of that Great American Novel you have been planning in your head for so long. How can you concentrate when all these thoughts, song lyrics, and odd bits of conversation jostle each other in your beleaguered brain? So, eventually, you just can't stand the experience of being chained to your chair for no apparent good reason, and off you go in search of distraction. You don't consciously intend to distract yourself, but your restlessness takes you on a tour of the house, where you naturally find all sorts of little jobs just begging for your attention. And the Great American Novel is, once again, put on the back burner.

A Way Around It—This was not written to point the finger of blame in your direction, but only to help you consider that the problem of distraction is more complex than simply one of dealing with noise from the outside. It may help your progress with that best-seller if you take your "house tours" to a more conscious level. Give yourself built-in breaks from that chair, but set a time limit for your wanderings. If all else fails, call a halt to your writing session and make a decision to do something that better suits your current mental state.

"It's pretty hard to be efficient without being obnoxious."
—*Kin Hubbard*

We don't know about you, but we have always been offended by bustling efficiency—mostly because we can't manage it ourselves. Many of those proficient people out there seem to be so conspicuous about checking off their lists of chores, errands, and appointments. Plus, they let it be known that they head up committees, attend all vital community meetings, and have people over for dinner weekly. It feels as if they are saying, "See how wonderful I am and what a worm you are."

And we believe them, because we never do anything in such a straight-line fashion. We fumble, we bumble, and we take a lot of breaks and detours to boot. Those of us who do manage to work up the head of steam we need to stay on task often become locomotives. We blow our whistle at every curve and intersection, and knock anyone off the tracks who gets in our way.

A Way Around It—Use strategies to keep yourself on track, but don't allow a given task to take on too much importance. In other words, if it's making you shove aside important people in your life, along with your own serenity, it's time to slow down. There is a lot more to life than efficiency.

"Always make sure your fly is zipped before you go on."
—*Al Lampkin*

When I leave for an appointment, I typically make five or six return trips back inside my house before I'm finally ready to leave. And, of course, these aren't leisurely walks to and fro. They are frantic fifty-yard dashes, with one eye on my watch.

Why do the hands on my watch move so damn fast when I'm in a hurry and so slowly when I'm, say, waiting for a refund check from the IRS? It is truly an inexplicable quirk of nature or something.

I have to tell the truth: I know that the hands don't really move any quicker . . . but I do run much faster than I used to. I have to. I have no choice because I'm frequently late! I think maybe I was born late and have been trying to catch up ever since. I guess that's not much of an excuse either, is it?

A Way Around It—It's easy to throw in the towel, giving up on the seemingly impossible dream of improving one's time management skills. Efforts in this regard may seem futile. Before you give up in frustration, however, remember that managing time is a skill and, as such, *can* be learned. While learning specific time management strategies is an invaluable skill, it is far from the entire answer. Instead, start by looking at your life balance sheet with an eye toward serious slicing and dicing, particularly of your "should-dos."

—P. R.

"I don't want to own anything that won't fit into my coffin."
　　　　　　　　　　　　　　　　　　　　—*Fred Allen*

Trying to pare down our possessions quite this much may not be realistic. But it's a far better goal to shoot for than the one inscribed on the T-shirt that proclaims, "The one who dies with the most toys wins!!"

If you check out the classified advertisements for yard sales, you'll conclude that lots of folks have garages and basements filled with unwanted miscellany. For many of us ADDers, though, accumulating too many castoffs can be deadly. It usually requires far more than a garage sale for us to escape from beneath mounds of disorganized stuff. And as if that weren't bad enough, we have assorted boxes of the latest and greatest gadgets we've impulsively bought.

It follows that the more we acquire, the more we'll have to organize—a difficult task for us. So, as we accumulate more things, we end up with more disorder to manage . . . and less time than we had before.

A Way Around It—Read the chapters about balance and organization in *You Mean I'm Not Lazy, Stupid or Crazy?!* In them you will find a variety of practical suggestions for paring down the mess and clutter in your life. And before you acquire new possessions, ask yourself if you are willing to pay the hidden costs: the expense to you in terms of your time, energy, and perhaps even your sanity!

"The volume of paper expands to fill the available briefcases."
                                                    —*Jerry Brown*

Ah, yes, the Paperwork Plague. You leave two pieces of paper on your desktop and by morning they have reproduced, creating an entire pile of new pieces of paper! A mystery, indeed.

Some ADDers don't seem to have undue difficulty managing the paper pile-ups in their lives, but many of us do. We don't throw things away, because we might need them sometime in the distant future. We don't put things away, because we can't figure out where to put them. And we know that out of sight is out of mind, so we don't dare file something away where we can't see it. This leads to another disorder comorbid with ADD—File Cabinet Phobia!

Just kidding, folks, we invented that one. You won't find it in any version of the *DSM*. That this problem is not officially recognized by the American Psychiatric Association doesn't mean that it isn't a real and serious problem, though.

A Way Around It—Is your trash can clean, shiny, and empty and your desktop covered from edge to edge with littered papers? If so, it's time for a major overhaul of your Paper Pile Management Operating System! A good way to start might be to try The Bigger the Box the Better Decluttering System. Grab your miscellany of papers, knicknacks, books, etc., and pack it all in one large box, taking care to leave out your current bills, speeding ticket, and anything else that *must* be handled ASAP. By eliminating the problem of indecision, you can experience instant gratification—viewing your desktop for the first time in years! The reduction of visual clutter also provides a "clean slate" from which you can begin your reorganization.

"The giraffe must get up at six in the morning if it wants
to have its breakfast in its stomach by nine."
—*Samuel Butler*

Perhaps that strategy works well for giraffes, but we're not
sure it was meant for human beings. Six in the morning is
an ungodly hour to drag yourself out of bed, especially
when you managed to crawl into it only three or four
hours earlier!

It's true that early mornings can be quiet and peaceful.
The chores don't have to be started yet, and the children
are still sleeping. The solitude allows you to think your
own thoughts, assuming that you have any this early in
the morning! And it's wonderful to have some extra
time to ease yourself into the day. There are those of us,
however, who simply "don't do mornings," no matter
what.

Everyone has their own biological time clock, a system
that controls daily cycles of energy and mental acuity.
For many people, these daily rhythms break down roughly
into five time periods: 9 A.M.–12 noon, high gear; 12–4
P.M., moderate alertness; 4–6 P.M., low gear; 6–10 P.M.,
nearly comatose; 10 P.M.–morning, rest/sleep. Your
biological clock may well be set differently. Many ADDers
don't really wake up until ten or eleven in the morning,
perhaps hitting peak performance sometime between
10 P.M. and 2 A.M. They don't call us night owls for
nothing!

A Way Around It—Before you can think about changing
your daily schedule to fit your biological rhythms, you
must determine how your personal performance time
clock operates. Take a little unscientific test. Try doing a
cognitive task, like a challenging crossword puzzle, in the
morning and again in the evening. When do you seem to

have a greater supply of mental fuel? When are you more clearheaded? Similarly, take a brisk five-minute walk in the morning and evening. At which time do you feel more invigorated . . . or exhausted?

"He pasted picture postcards around goldfish bowls to make the goldfish think they were going places."

—*Fred Allen*

What a kind gesture—creating a pleasant environment for one's fish! This could also be an effective antiboredom technique, I suppose. And how about procrastination? *Sorry I let the car's registration expire . . . I was just too busy redecorating the fishbowl!*

I've engaged in similar behavior during what used to be my twice-weekly office reorganizing sessions. I vividly remember Kate's consternation at discovering me on my hands and knees painting my desk gray with red polka dots. (I was supposed to be editing our first book.) At the time, my actions seemed completely logical to me: I couldn't start working until my environment *felt* right. Of course, when the painting was finished, I simply had to improve my desktop organization and attack my files, which involved trying out a new system every few days. I took color coding to a new level of complexity. Red, yellow, blue, and green file folders weren't enough, so I'd color manila folders with markers, resulting in a filing system divided into twelve or fifteen different categories. Confusion reigned supreme as I racked my brain, trying to remember such a complicated and ever-evolving system. Not a problem, however—I'd simply invent an indexing system on a sheet of paper to manage my filing system! And so it went, one system replaced by another equally unusable one. At least I didn't repaint the desk; it's still gray with red polka dots.

A Way Around It—It is important to create a pleasant work environment. Painting a wall in a bright, cheerful color or hanging inspirational posters can provide ongoing encouragement. And it is equally important to replace a Paper Pile Procedure with a more efficient filing system. Just don't go overboard or what you'll really be doing is procrastinating. Aim for simplicity in designing your work environment, keeping your efforts firmly focused on your goal—improved productivity.

—P. R.

"I have a microwave fireplace. You can lay down in front
  of the fire all night in eight minutes."
                                              —*Stephen Wright*

This quote seems to capture the reality of life in the late
twentieth century. We seem to spend our lives hurrying
up the pace of our lives! Mail can be sent in milliseconds
through cyberspace all around the world. Dinner is prepared in minutes in our microwave ovens. Cross-country
travel can be accomplished in a few hours. Think about
the technological breakthroughs of recent years.
Virtually all of them have been designed to increase
the speed with which we can accomplish various life
endeavors.

   With the ability to do so many things so much more
quickly than in the past, we should be enjoying the
extra time that technology has freed up for us. But that's
not what has really happened, is it? If anything, we feel
more frazzled than before because we just keep filling in
the newly available time with more to-dos. We may
have changed the equation, but we have little to show
for it except an ever-growing feeling that we should be
doing more, not less. If you are carefully scheduling your
days and still feeling out of control, you may be focusing
on details at the expense of the larger picture of your
life.

A *Way Around It*—It may be time to do some values clar-
ification. To refine your thinking, try this exercise. Imagine yourself ten years from now, describing your life as you
wish it to be. Think about all five areas of life's goals:
spiritual, family/relationships, mental/educational,
social/recreational, and financial. What do you want to
be remembered for; what kind of parent, friend, or spouse

do you want to be; what's really important to you? Focusing on these life goals may help you to reduce the insignificant to-dos in your daily life, resulting in more quality time for yourself.

8

Learning
and
Memory

When we think of learning, we often equate it with academic education—the operations we learned in math courses and the names, dates, and places we memorized, or were supposed to memorize(!) in various courses throughout our years in school. This is a limited view, however, of learning and its integrally related partner, memory. Learning isn't merely a collection of information. It is, instead, a realization of something that actually changes behavior, either internally or externally or both. All our thoughts and the actions that follow are learned. This includes specific knowledge as well as habits, defense mechanisms, social conventions, communication skills, problem-solving techniques . . . ad infinitum. Everything that is learned can be unlearned, although unlearning, say, a bad habit, is actually more effortful than learning it in the first place, because each time we focus on the unwanted behavior, we unknowingly reinforce it.

Anything that is noted is learned when attention is focused long enough to be stored in memory. Thus, attention, memory, and learning are all essential components of an interrelated operational system. When we learn something, what we've done is manage to transfer what we've noted to the storage vaults of long-term memory. This can be a difficult process, given the ADDer's tendency to jump impulsively from one thing to another. If the learning process begins with erratic attention to details, it follows that the quality of learning, i.e., memory, will be negatively affected. When we say that we've forgotten something, what we're actually saying is that we never adequately learned it in the first place. We may have attended to something, but not long enough or carefully enough for it to register in our brains. So, our learning problems are our memory problems, which are our learning problems . . . well, you probably get the picture.

Learning and memory difficulties seem to plague many of us, the symptom of distractibility playing a major role in them. The fact is, however, that everyone has varied strengths and weaknesses regarding individual differences in learning and memory capacities. Clearly, innate intelligence—the venerable IQ—plays a part, but as pioneers like Howard Gardner postulate, there are many more kinds of intelligences than those of performance and verbal skills measured by standardized IQ tests. Gardner submits that human beings have seven different learning modes, his theory of "multiple intelligences" encompassing logical/mathematical, verbal/linguistic, visual/spatial, intrapersonal/interpersonal, body/kinesthetic, and musical/rhythmic.

In addition, researcher Dr. Anthony F. Gregorc has identified four types of Mindstyles®, each with its own specific characteristics, strengths, limitations, and frustrations: concrete sequential, abstract sequential, concrete random, and abstract random. And from the professional circle of education specialists comes a parallel theory that each of us has a preferred sensory learning channel or unique combination thereof: visual, auditory, kinesthetic/haptic (relating to the sense of touch), or multisensory. And then there's the perhaps better-known right brain/left brain theory of learning that originated with the Nobel Prize–winning work of Roger Sperry of the California Institute of Technology. Sperry, along with Robert Ornstein, famed for his work on brain waves and specialization of brain functions, discovered that each of the two hemispheres of the brain—the left and right cortices—deals with different types of mental activity. Although a complete examination of these fascinating emerging theories of memory and learning is beyond the scope of this book, suffice it to say that whatever your long-standing beliefs about your ability—or inability—to learn and remember, they are probably incomplete and overly critical.

Perhaps the most accurate way to characterize our respective learning and memory capacities is to identify and describe our weaknesses as areas of potential that have not yet been nourished and our strengths as those we have already successfully developed. This will be the underlying "philosophy" of the following section of this book as we contemplate the mystery of the *biocomputer* that is the brain, exploring and honoring the unique differences and often untapped and unrecognized talents of us ADDers.

"Get to know what it is you don't know as fast as you can."
—*Robert Heller*

One problem with accomplishing this is that those of us with ADD have a lifelong pattern of hiding what we don't know from those around us. We spend our lives surrounded by people who seem to know it all and to be in perfect control of every situation. On one level, we are aware that those people are just wearing a mask of competence; nobody has it all together. But those facades fool us nonetheless, causing us to doubt ourselves, and making it difficult for us to admit that we need to learn.

It has been hard for me to be honest about the many things I don't know without feeling bad about myself. I began by telling a supportive person about some of the little things I never learned, and asking them to help me learn the skills—tasks such as mopping the floor, doing the laundry, and ironing my clothes. The person who taught me was patient and didn't make me feel like an idiot because I was all grown up and still didn't know how to do these things. Having a positive learning experience enabled me, step by step, to begin admitting to many of the other skills I needed to learn.

A Way Around It—Take an inventory of yourself, considering honestly what you know, what you don't know, and what you think is necessary for you to learn. Pay little attention to the quote at the top of the page; it was just a jumping-off place for my thoughts. The process of assessing your knowledge and skill gaps and then remediating them can't be done quickly. It takes time. Most likely you will be learning little bits and pieces as you go along. Remember that the first step is finding the courage to admit that you don't know a lot of the things you think you should already have learned.
—D. S. L.

"There's never time to do it right, but always time to do it over."

—*John Meckiman*

We've heard this one all too often from parents, teachers, and bosses: "If you would only take the time to do it right in the first place, you wouldn't have to do it over." The problem is that ADDults often need a lot of repetition in order to learn. Now, I don't know about you, but it has always been hard for me to do the same tasks over and over until I get them right. I feel dumb because everyone else seems to be able to learn a skill after only one or two attempts.

To cover up my feelings of inadequacy, I have often faked my way through a task, knowing that I wasn't doing it quite right, but afraid of taking the time to really master it because I thought other people would not respect me if they saw that I wasn't up to speed. These days I am working hard to stop belittling myself because I learn differently. I know I deserve the right to learn and perform in my way, at my own pace.

A Way Around It—Doing your personal best should be your guiding rule, not the amount of time or number of repetitions required for the learning process. Look for small indicators of progress as you work at gaining a new skill. With each repetition, focus on the improvements you have made since the last attempt, instead of the mistakes.

—D. S. L.

"He who is afraid of asking is afraid of learning."

—*Danish proverb*

When I talk with ADD teens about school and the information presented in class, I find that there are usually huge gaps in their understanding. The responses to my initial question—"Why didn't you ask the teacher to explain it to you again?"—are typically, "The teacher doesn't like me," or "I'm afraid of getting in trouble again." Part of me gets a bit irritated by these comments, knowing that they accomplish nothing but getting in the way of learning. Much as I want to impart my greater wisdom about the importance of taking responsibility for one's own learning, I usually manage to resist the urge to preach. Because the truth is, I understand exactly how these teens feel. I recognize the comments for what they are—excuses. The same kinds of excuses I made during those long years of trying to learn in school . . . and failing again and again. The only difference between those students and me is that they lack the decades of painful experiences that have taught me that making excuses—assigning blame to others—just gets in the way of my own learning.

Though I know intellectually that asking for help is essential to the learning process, I don't always *practice what I preach*. Putting lofty principles into practice is often easier contemplated than accomplished. I confess that I am still afraid of asking questions when I don't understand something, especially in the workplace. The issue of disclosure is a real dilemma—if I stop faking it, I and my ADD might be found out. In spite of recent advances regarding the rights of employees with disabilities, I know that many of us ADDers continue to feel hesitant about doing anything that might reveal our disability to employers. We are afraid of losing our jobs, getting passed over for promotions, or being reassigned to simple, mindless, repetitious tasks. And, regrettably, provisions of the Americans with Disabilities Act notwithstanding, the decision to disclose one's ADD continues to be one fraught with frightening unknowns.

A Way Around It—Fear is a natural human response, but it can seriously interfere with the learning process. In addition, trying to hide your weaknesses from an employer won't work for long. Even if you choose not to disclose your ADD, it is still better to admit your learning gaps as you demonstrate your willingness to work at gaining the requisite skills. You will gain points with your employer if you wait until he or she is finished talking before politely asking your questions and sticking to the current topic. Taking detailed notes can also save both you and your employer from the ordeal of endlessly repeating the same questions and answers.

—D. S. L.

"Thank you for sending me a copy of your book. I'll waste no time in reading it."

—*Anonymous*

Many of our friends and acquaintances have been harboring a guilty secret: They confess that they've never quite gotten around to reading *You Mean I'm Not Lazy, Stupid or Crazy?!* They know they have ADD and are quite sure that the book would be helpful. "If only I could bring myself to sit down and actually read the darn thing," the ADDer says somewhat apologetically. As if this seeming lack of interest is offensive! It's not. Not even a little. It also evokes not the slightest surprise. Having ADD means having many unfinished tasks, some of which never even get started! And it means that those that are somehow finished are typically completed much later than intended or desired.

On top of that, many an adult with ADD would rather endure unimaginable physical torture than submit to the ordeal of reading a book. Unfortunately, we ADDers have absorbed the erroneous message that reading quickly and well is an indicator of one's intelligence. But reading is simply one of several channels that convey information to the brain. Listening to tapes, watching videos, or learning experientially are equally valuable tools for expanding our knowledge.

A Way Around It—Stop beating yourself up if you're not a great reader. Do try to exercise your brain and strengthen your skills by reading at least occasionally. For the most part, though, find, strengthen, and use your strongest learning channels, whatever they are.

"The left hemisphere became the one to have if you were having only one."

—Howard Gardner

Actually, this left brain/right brain business is an inaccurate and incomplete method for describing the working of individual minds. Nobody is a completely concrete, linear (left-brain) or abstract, creative (right-brain) learner. People simply have stronger tendencies toward one of these two thinking styles, and everyone uses both for certain tasks. It is true, though, that those who tend toward the right hemisphere, which many ADDers do, seem to be disadvantaged in our society.

Folks who "lean to the left" have a sequential, orderly thinking style that provides a good fit with many of the demands of both the academic and work worlds. Society at large values the strengths of this thinking style, frequently rewarding "left brainers" with well-paying jobs and stellar academic careers. That the largely abstract, creative right-brain style is less valued is evidenced by our culture's not-so-great track record at supporting the arts and by such things as school boards' fiscal policies in their regard: Art and music courses are frills, the first courses to be cut when money gets tight. And parents aren't immune from "leaning left," traditionally breathing a sigh of relief when Junior chooses the safer, more socially acceptable occupation of accounting, education, business, or medicine rather than the elusive and less financially secure professional life of a writer, actor, or musician.

The fact is, though, that the world has changed radically in recent years. No vocation is safe from the ravages of downsizing. Entire categories of jobs are becoming obsolete overnight, victims of the massive upheavals that accompany the shift from an industrial society to the information age. The final result of this painful transition, however, may be freedom from excessive left-brain thinking. If there is no longer any job security, we may opt for riskier routes, ones that nurture the souls of us freewheeling thinkers rather than stifling them.

A Way Around It—Look for balance as you organize your lifestyle. Prepare yourself by developing a set of skills valuable in a variety of work settings, such as computer literacy and an effective communication style. Exercise the muscles of your less dominant hemisphere. For example, if your lifestyle leans strongly toward the chaotic and creative, become involved in a hobby or activity that is structured. If you have leaned too far in the other direction, loosen up a bit by trying some activities that require improvisation.

"When I first went into the active army, you could tell someone to move a chair across the room—now you have to tell him why."

—*Maj. Robert Lembke*

We can relate to the frustrations experienced by both parties in this type of transaction. With our short ADD fuses, it takes all of our patience to give step-by-step instructions without having to explain the whys, too. It is especially difficult if one has to do it more than once or very slowly. When we have been in teaching positions, for example, each of us has found ourself getting very irritable when carefully planned lectures were interrupted by students' questions.

In spite of our own need to know the reason behind directions, we don't want to deal with the same curiosity in others. Their questions just get in the way of our goals. We realize, though, that a manner too brisk or brusque won't gain the cooperation of others any more than it does ours. It's a new world out there, and barking commands just doesn't work. Not that we ADDers ever responded well to orders in the first place.

A Way Around It—When you find yourself getting irritated at having to repeat instructions, take a deep breath, count to ten if you need to, and remember what it feels like to be told to do something without explanation. You may even save yourself a few repetitions by exercising patience.

"Our memories are card indexes consulted, and then put back in disorder by authorities whom we do not control."
—*Cyril Connolly*

Yes, our memories are slippery and rebellious things, like toddlers who lead us on a merry chase, laughing in glee as they give us the slip. When we go on a mission up there in our heads, hell-bent on retrieving some fact or stored experience, the filing system becomes incomprehensible. The vast jumble of stuff simply overwhelms us. And the harder we try, the more confusing and frustrating it gets.

Sometimes one can actually consult one's memory. But more often than not, it is quite obvious that we are not in charge of the process. For example, strange and irrelevant thoughts intrude at the darnedest times. They make us wonder where so much junk comes from and why it has to hang around cluttering up our minds. The problem is, we can't just decide what to keep and what to throw away. Even then we need the courage to pitch the garbage. Someone should develop an efficient method of mental hygiene and market it. They would definitely make a bundle.

A Way Around It—Resist the tendency to use overzealous memory aids and systems. There will always be disorder up there. Compulsive attempts to clean and straighten will only waste your time and make you cranky. However, do devise your own methods to remember appointments and people's names, for the sake of civility. But don't sweat the small stuff. Keep in mind that if you try to grab at a memory, it will almost always disappear. But if you give it a rest, it often floats to the surface.

"I think I committed the ADD faux pas of the century. My husband's sister died and her husband called with the bad news. Two days later, I remembered the message I had forgotten to write down, and I had to figure out a way to tell my husband that, by the way, his sister had died a couple of days ago."

—*M. J. Johnson*

This really happened to our dear friend M. J. The reactions of those hearing the story have been interesting—and mixed. Folks with ADD laugh, nodding in recognition that "there but for the grace of God go I." Those with little or no understanding of ADD are shocked, both by the accompanying laughter of ADDers and by the incident itself. How could this woman possibly forget something of such great import? they wonder.

But we ADDers know all too well how something like this can happen. Our problems with memory are often serious and debilitating. It is a fact that strong emotions help to fix events in the memory. This is true for everyone but is even more critical for people with ADD, whose erratic attention creates recall problems. Without a close relationship and deep connection to her sister-in-law, M. J. likely lacked the highly charged emotional anchor needed to secure the information in long-term memory. Further, any number of concurring experiences may well have been competing for her attention and capacity to remember. It wasn't a failure of caring enough on her part; it was the way the ADD mind works.

A Way Around It—Forgive yourself your trespasses related to memory, but do come up with a way to compensate for this deficiency. Do not rely on your memory alone when it comes to relaying important messages. Instead, take the time to write the information down, placing the note where it will be seen. Or use one of the new recording devices. They're small, inexpensive, and convenient. Make a habit of listening to your recorded message, at least daily.

"Stand firm in your refusal to remain conscious in algebra. In real life, I assure you, there is no such thing as algebra."
—*Fran Lebowitz*

In general, I agree with this point of view. There are so many elements in our schools' curricula that make little or no sense. Take cursive writing, for example. My handwriting is much worse than any physician's scrawl I ever saw, yet it hasn't hampered me in any important way. To tell you the truth, once I got past the nuns in elementary school, I gave up cursive writing for good. I knew that I would never get any better at it, and so I didn't see any point in cramping my hand and my brain anymore.

Thanks to the invention of word processing, you can get by just fine as long as you can manage to scribble your signature on important documents, such as checks. Or print legibly and quickly enough to read your own handwriting when you take notes in class. Of course, you can bypass that one by recording the lecture.

As far as the algebra goes, I found that there really was a practical use for the darn stuff. In nursing, we use algebra daily to make calculations related to medication doses—not something you want to be casual about. They won't let you *out* of nursing school without solid skills in algebra. My basic point is that everyone does not need the same set of skills, and if someone needs or wants a skill badly enough, motivation can overcome a handicap.

A Way Around It—If a requirement for a degree or program seems irrelevant, question it. You may not get immediate action—in fact, you probably won't. And you also may discover that there is actually a purpose behind it. If it really isn't necessary, a large chorus of voices saying the same thing can eventually effect change.
—K. K.

"For every person wishing to teach, there are thirty not wanting to be taught."

—Anonymous

Let's see here. Does this mean that students are the bad guys, making it impossible for instructors to teach them anything? Does it mean that teachers are the villains, turning eager students into unwilling, unenthusiastic learners? Or does it mean both? The correct answer is: none of the above! The problem probably doesn't lie with the teacher or the student but in the method used to get the job done: the lecture! Few learn well, regardless of whether or not they have ADD, by listening to the dull drone of a teacher, but many teachers think they have to do it this way because it's the way they were taught to teach. Unfortunately, with the lecture method, the learner is primarily engaged in an endurance contest, trying to stay awake, quiet, and still, the only stimulation coming from the irritant of the teacher's drone. Having been on the other side of the lectern, we confess that as teachers and workshop presenters, we have often bored *ourselves* silly reciting from canned lecture notes—but we are mending our ways!

A Way Around It— Listen to that inner voice telling you that this lecture business is hogwash. Refuse to teach or be taught by these archaic methods, and insist on your right to be an active participant in the learning process.

"You must realize that honorary degrees are given generally to people whose SAT scores were too low to get
them into schools the regular way. As a matter of fact, it
was my SAT scores that led me into my present vocation
in life—comedy."

—*Neil Simon*

Another nail in the coffin of these standardized tests—
people getting honorary degrees for excelling in at least
one field. It doesn't matter that they couldn't jump
through the hoop of a paper-and-pencil test. I know these
tests are a scam because I am one of those people who perform brilliantly on them. And my high scores have nothing to do with my grasp of the subject matter, diligent
study, or ability to actually *do* anything in the area being
tested. I just have a gift for taking those tests—a gift that
has saved my behind more than once.

My SAT scores got me a provisional acceptance to college, for instance, when my grades were pretty much in
the toilet. Of course, I had to work hard playing catch-up
and learning to function in a more practical sense. I also
did learn how to get good grades eventually.

Those As were nice, but they didn't help me organize
my hospital work as a nursing student. I discovered that
many of the students who struggled with tests were wonderful nurses, much better than I was. The tests were only
a ticket of admission and a prop for a fragile self-esteem
during those times when the real-life tests were overwhelming. I did finally master the practical skills in nursing school, with the patient help of an instructor who saw
past the high marks to the frightened person inside.

A Way Around It—Refuse to measure your worth by the
yardstick of test scores. They are less than meaningless.

But don't look a gift horse in the mouth, either, if you happen to be one of those people who can ace them. As ADDers, we need all the help we can get. In the meantime, become an activist in the fight to obtain a more useful and just way to measure achievement, academic or otherwise.

—K. K.

"I love computers, but I wish that my entire computerized record-keeping and appointment setup at my HMO, and in general, would flag my accounts with WARNING! ADD: THIS PERSON NEEDS EXPLICIT INSTRUCTIONS AND EXTRA REMINDERS."
—*Julia Smith-Ruetz*

And so do we. It is so humiliating to have to ask for the same information for the tenth time. In all fairness, in many cases it isn't our fault, because the information is incomplete to begin with. This is especially true when it comes to our health care system, supposedly one of the best in the world. We know there are many competent and caring health care professionals who are just as frustrated by bureaucratic snafus as the consumer who is caught up in those glitches.

If the system is a chaotic mess difficult to navigate even for those armed with information and savvy, you can imagine how hard it becomes when you have ADD gumming up the works. You forget that appointment it took you weeks or months to make. And you are frustrated by the rules, such as the one requiring monthly prescriptions for stimulant medication. You have enough trouble remembering to take the darn stuff to begin with. Is it really necessary to have to run the gauntlet every month on top of it? First, the round of phone tag with your doctor to get a refill. Then he or she forgets to note that you can't take generic Ritalin. And then your HMO says that your doctor has to prescribe the generic, to cut costs. And around and around you go. Every single month!

A Way Around It—Arm yourself with as much information as you can. Realize that the health care system is chaotic and confusing territory for everyone, even the professionals who work within it. Try to find doctors and pharmacists you can trust to help you circumvent the problems whenever possible. And remember, although it may be a difficult act to pull off, a smiling, assertive manner will go much further than an impatient, hostile one.

> "But my answer's not the right one
> Though I did my very best,
> For overnight, they changed the rules
> I studied for the test."
>
> —*Peter S. Latham*

It seems as if the rules are always changing. All the rules, not just the ones for those paper-and-pencil tests. So, for those of us with ADD, the area of social behavior is a minefield. But nobody knows how to behave anymore. Leaders from all fields, along with the man or woman on the street, hotly debate the issue of what it means to "do the right thing." Even Emily Post would be confused in this environment. There is no gold standard for behavior anymore.

Those old books on wedding etiquette, for example, don't have any guidelines for including the bride and groom's new baby in the ceremony. And they offer no help to anyone in charge of planning a same-sex wedding. Even getting dressed is an ordeal, whatever the occasion. Casual dress means just about anything and everything, so no matter how carefully you plan your outfit to blend in with the crowd, you may end up sticking out like a sore thumb. So how are we with ADD to negotiate in such a chaotic environment? We have trouble enough with simple and clear-cut rules.

A Way Around It—It is okay to be different, as long as you don't trample on others' rights or feelings in so doing. Just because the rules of "proper" behavior are up for grabs doesn't mean that the rules of "caring" behavior need to go out of style, too. Etiquette was invented to help people treat each other with kindness and respect. Let us make that our new gold standard.

> "I don't remember anybody's name. Why do you think the 'dahling' thing started?"
>
> —*Zsa Zsa Gabor*

The ADD memory is a tricky thing. We all suffer from some form of memory impairment, but it takes a different form in each of us. Some of us can't remember names, while others forget phone numbers, sometimes even our own. To complicate things further, the things we are good at remembering tend to fade in and out without warning.

Take the name problem, for example. We can be perfectly adequate at remembering names, until the pressure is on at a formal social occasion, when we find ourselves groping for a name that refuses to rise to the tip of the tongue—especially when the person we are supposed to introduce is the boss's wife, or our neighbor of twenty years.

There are as many quirky memory glitches as there are people on the planet, but it does seem that the name problem causes the most guilt and embarrassment, because most people assume—erroneously—that forgetting a name is a sign that you don't value the person whose name you have forgotten. In reality, though, one may remember many details about another person and still have trouble recalling their name.

A Way Around It—Calling someone "dahling" or "honey" or even "yo" is one way to handle the elusive name problem, but that strategy will ultimately backfire. Most people feel that they are not very important or unique when addressed in this fashion. It's much better simply to fess up to your memory problem. Also, you will have a better chance of being forgiven if you manage to slip some flattering details you have remembered about that person into the conversation.

"You cannot make a crab walk straight."

— *Aristophanes*

Trying to force a crab to walk straight makes as much sense as trying to force someone to learn. Unfortunately, that's exactly what goes on in too many classrooms, where teachers give lectures to students who are expected to learn by absorbing the pearls of wisdom falling from those instructors' mouths.

Many of us spent years in classrooms like these, our education consisting of little more than daily exercises in memorization. It wouldn't be fair, however, to blame the teachers; some were dedicated educators in the best sense of the word. The educational system simply wasn't designed for students unable to learn by listening. It definitely wasn't prepared to handle the special needs of students such as us.

Remember that the academic failure you may have experienced wasn't because you were *lazy, stupid, or crazy*—it was the result of a disorder you didn't know you had. So if you are considering going back to school, don't let your past experiences stop you. You know about your ADD now and are learning strategies to manage the symptoms that had created obstacles to your academic success. And there's something else to keep in mind. As an ADDult, you don't have to accept educational mediocrity, sitting idly by while an instructor engages in the "force a crab to walk straight" teaching model. You have a voice and can advocate for your right to learn in the way that works best for you.

A Way Around It—Each of us has a natural learning style—a preferred way of thinking, remembering, and learning. Figure out what your style is—do you learn best by seeing? hearing? doing? All three together? Then, experiment with various strategies that work well for the kind of learner you are. You don't have to invent them. There are many excellent books loaded with tips and tricks for different learning styles.

"Follow the rules of holes: If you are in one, stop digging."
—*Dennis Healy*

Habits are behavioral patterns that, with time and use, have become automatic. Golfers and tennis players refer to their learned stroking techniques as grooves. As on a record, an ever-deepening groove is made in the motor memory brain cells each time a particular action is performed. After a while, the groove becomes sufficiently deep that the record player's needle, as it were, falls into it automatically. And voilà!—habits are created. Good ones . . . and bad ones.

Popular wisdom tells us that if you've learned a "bad" habit, you ought to be able simply to unlearn it. Just because a notion is popular, however, doesn't mean it is necessarily wise. Think about it—how is it possible just to erase those deeply etched grooves, in a record or in the brain?

Most of us have bad habits we have tried to break. But the harder we try to break the habit through sheer willpower, the worse it gets. We become so focused on the behavior we're trying to change that we become obsessed with it, never considering that there are other behaviors we could substitute for it. That's the Catch-22 of Habits and Murphy's Law of Holes: Trying to dig yourself out of a hole just makes a bigger hole and a more deeply entrenched habit!

A Way Around It—Babies don't break their habit of crawling when they learn to walk. They simply leave one learned behavior behind, replacing it with another that gets them where they're going faster! Rather than pitching a headlong battle against an old habit, choose a replacement for it instead. Why work so hard at unlearning a response, beating yourself up about your lack of willpower, when it's more effective to substitute a new behavioral pattern?

9

Stress

For ADDers, stress is both the great motivator and the great enemy. A little bit of it, just the right amount, can give our brain chemicals the extra juice they need to put our often sluggish minds on alert. Stress, however, becomes our foe when it exerts too much force, pushing us into a mental red alert zone, where the knee-jerk reactions of the fight or flight response take over.

The fight or flight reaction is useful in some situations. It was especially helpful when most of us lived in jungles or caves, spending our time hunting for food and trying to avoid being eaten by predators. But, as pointed out by John-Roger and Peter McWilliams in their book *You Can't Afford the Luxury of a Negative Thought,* "In the past few hundred years—in the Western world, at least—the need for the Fight or Flight response has, for all practical purposes, disappeared."

Some of us, however, have become addicted to stress, using it as a drug to keep our brains and bodies going long past the point where they are screaming "uncle." Of course, some of the stressful events and situations we encounter are not under our control. Other stressors, though, are the result of out-of-control lifestyles that feed our addiction in insidious ways.

When you are in the throes of a bad stress habit, it is hard to tell the forest from the trees. You become so accustomed to reacting in emergency mode that you lose the habit of thinking before taking action. We fail to stop and ask such important questions as "Is this my emergency or someone else's?" or "Can I really do something about this problem? If so, do I have to do it *right now?*"

Another problem associated with chronic overuse of the fight or flight response is that it really does a number on your body. Most of the diseases that plague Western society are largely stress induced. In addition to all the specific health problems created by chronic stress, it also wreaks havoc with your body's feedback system. In a healthy, functioning human body, messages are sent to your brain from the other organs of your body, letting you know how things are going down there. Your stomach signals that you are hungry, while your muscles inform you with messages of discomfort when they have had enough.

The fight or flight response, however, is designed to override the messages signaling pain, hunger, and fatigue. It is a handy feature, really, because it acts to marshal your body's energy for a battle or a hasty retreat. It is not helpful to be consumed with a desire for fast food during a high-speed chase on the highway, for example. When you live your life in high-stress mode, though, your feedback system stops working. You no longer know when you are hungry or in pain, because the messenger system is just limping along, crippled with overuse. Not only that, but you have now forgotten how to attend to and read the signals that *do* manage to reach your brain.

In this section, we are offering food for thought in regard to your personal relationship with stress. Are you a user, an abuser, or have you slid over the line into addiction? Of course, we all need a little excitement now and then; a totally stress-free existence is not desirable or attainable, at least this side of the grave. Your goal is to learn to assess and monitor the stress level in your life, gradually reducing stressors to obtain a healthier balance.

"Don't let life discourage you; everyone who got where he is had to begin where he was."

—*R. L. Evans*

How easy it is to become preoccupied with where we want to be instead of where we are. We look at all the successful, happy, "normal" people out there and wish we were walking in their shoes. Or at least we think it would be a pretty good deal. Without actually being able to crawl into someone else's life, it's hard to tell if it is all that it seems to be. The happiness may be just an illusion, and the normalcy certainly is. We have never met anyone who was entirely "normal"; have you?

As for success, when we view successful people, we are seeing only the finished product, so to speak. The hurdles they jumped and the gritty struggles they went through are not in evidence. This makes it hard to visualize ourselves getting to the same place. The success thing becomes something magical, hard to translate into everyday action, when you only see the happily-ever-after part of the story. In reality, every person who ever distinguished themself had to take it one small step at a time, hanging in there and dealing with many setbacks along the way.

A Way Around It—The first step is accepting that where you are now is okay. You need your energy for setting and achieving your goals. Don't waste it yearning to be something you are not. When you let go of the intense desire to be that ideal person in your mind's eye, it can open the door to possibilities you never imagined.

"A smile is a curved line that sets things straight."

—*Anonymous*

Remembering to smile is important. Nobody wants to hang around with someone who projects nothing but worry, or gloom and doom. Even the chronically grumpy souls out there don't want to spend a lot of time with people like themselves. Life is filled with stress, especially for those of us with ADD, but when we focus too much on the problems and challenges confronting us every day, we lose touch with important parts of ourselves.

When I first started to work on correcting my ADD behaviors, my son said I resembled Mr. Spock of *Star Trek*. I became computerlike, showing very little emotion. He was right. Because I was watching everything I said and did so closely, I had forgotten to smile. I was working so hard at observing myself that I lost the ability to feel and interact spontaneously with others. My son made me realize that I needed to lighten up, to stop taking this ADD recovery business so deadly seriously. I was trying to attack my problems with too much vengeance, thinking that I could make them vanish overnight if I just concentrated hard enough.

A Way Around It—You can't transform yourself instantly. But you can set small goals and work at them on a daily basis. Pay attention to your stress level and the body language signals you are sending out. If your facial muscles are setting into a frown of worry or concentration or your body is full of tension, stop yourself. Try to make a joke about your tendency to take everything too seriously. And smile. It doesn't take that much time or energy, and it helps ease everyone's tension.

—D. S. L.

"If you haven't all the things you want, be grateful for the things you don't have that you didn't want."

—*Anonymous*

We carry many burdens that we never wanted or asked for: people who don't understand us, employers who give us a hard time, and spouses who drive us crazy with demands that we measure up. But it could be a lot worse. Think of all the terrible diseases and catastrophes that could happen—the ones you don't have. Not a subject for pleasant daydreaming, but it may help put things in perspective.

ADD is not even close to what some people have to struggle with, and we even come with a set of built-in blessings to work with. We have great imaginations and a zest for life. We are creative and able to figure out unique solutions to problems. ADDults are usually fun to be with and willing to try new things on a minute's notice. These gifts can help us accept who we are and what we have.

A *Way Around It*—Take a mental inventory of the blessings in your life and write them down. Put the list on your refrigerator or on a wall where you will see it frequently. If you can't for the life of you come up with any positives, make a list of all the horrible things you can imagine that you don't have or that have never happened to you. Whenever you find yourself sinking into a negative frame of mind, read your list for a quick pick-me-up.

"Nothing will ever be attempted if all possible objections must be first overcome."

—*Dr. Samuel Johnson*

We will always encounter obstacles when it comes to realizing our dreams. When we look at them all at once, it is overwhelming. How can we possibly work our way to a goal when we have to bushwhack our way through all those problems and details first? That long history of failure does a spontaneous instant replay in our heads when we encounter obstacles. It can be tempting to give up at the starting gate when we anticipate the challenges and the energy-sapping fears that go along with them.

For that matter, everyday life is a challenge for us. The word *challenge* conjures up grand visions of climbing Mt. Everest or swimming the English Channel. For learning-challenged adults, keeping up with appointments, commitments, phone numbers, or details is the psychological equivalent of trekking up that daunting mountain. We don't get any awards or positive press for it, either. Under the circumstances, it is all too easy to give up, to succumb to bitterness and despair, to believe that life is too hard for us to cope with, and spend our time ruminating about the raw deal we were given.

A Way Around It—Don't forget that grand vision of conquering some great challenge, your personal equivalent of Everest. But do keep it firmly in mind that this is a long-term goal. The strength to keep going comes from the small successes of everyday life. When the words "I can't" creep into your thoughts, replace them with a new and better mantra, such as "I haven't figured out how to do it yet, but I'm working on it and I know I can do this."

"Did you hear what the white rat said to the other white rat? . . . I've got that psychologist so well trained that every time I ring the bell he brings me something to eat."
—*David Mercer*

Recalling this joke may help when you feel like a guinea pig, when the people you are looking to for help seem to be jerking you around and experimenting on you. It is hard not to feel that way, because at this stage of the game, the ADD thing is a voyage into the unknown. There are no experts. None of us knows enough, and we are all shooting in the dark.

But we don't want to lead you to despair. It is possible to participate in an experiment with a reasonable level of safety, dignity, and input into the process. And since there is always some trial and error in each individual's treatment plan, you should expect and demand that your helping professionals outline the choices, including both risks and benefits. They should listen to your questions carefully and treat your knowledge and ideas with the respect they deserve.

A Way Around It—Don't forget that you have the ultimate control and the last say when it comes to your mind and body. However, you don't want to control the entire process, because then there would be no benefit in consulting someone else for help. Instead, strive to build balance and a partnership in your relationships with helping professionals.

"I can't play guitar and sing at the same time. My brain can't handle it. I can't even play rhythm guitar and sing. It's hard enough for me to stay in tune just singing."

—*Frank Zappa*

This sums up a big chunk of our experiences as ADDults. And as children with ADD as well. In the past, however, the inability to walk and chew gum at the same time was more obvious to others. With the increased awareness that came with adolescence and young adulthood, we learned to hide our disability and narrow our sights to avoid the confusion of multitasking and the ensuing humiliation.

Many ADDers say they are great at multitasking, that that is the only way they keep themselves awake and alert. At home they talk on the phone, cook a meal, and deal with the children's battles at the same time. At the office they thrive on working at several projects simultaneously. Now, this doesn't happen to be the style that works for any of the three of us. After years of treatment and self-help, though, each of us is getting better at this. However, if one task or stressor too many is added, performance starts to unravel.

A *Way Around It*—As you progress in your ADD recovery, test and challenge your abilities from time to time. Your capacity to do more complicated tasks simultaneously should increase, but it will not be an overnight phenomenon. To avoid excessive stress and public embarrassment, attempt new challenges in private, or among good friends.

"When I was a child what I wanted to be when I grew up was an invalid."

—*Quentin Crisp*

A strange and perhaps pathetic ambition, but it strikes a chord. During those times when many of us have felt shrunken to almost nothing, beaten down by failure after failure, the wish to give up and be taken care of was very strong. Unconsciously, we often magnified and extended minor illnesses in order to justify a temporary retreat from life. It may well be that our minds actually pushed our bodies into illness some of those times. No one, including ourselves, knew or understood that our struggles were with a real disability—ADD. Being sick was the only excuse many of us could use to escape the unbearable stress.

A Way Around It—Acknowledge the feelings of helplessness and neediness that surface from time to time. They may be more intense when you have ADD, but they are just normal feelings that all humans experience. Don't be afraid to share them with a good friend. It's amazing how feelings lose their power to make you ill, or control you, when you expose them to the light of day.

"There is the greatest practical benefit in making a few failures early in life."

—*T. H. Huxley*

We agree wholeheartedly, having recognized the benefits of early failure in our own lives. After hitting rock bottom in adolescence, we were forced to look at ourselves with a critical eye. It is only now, in adulthood, that we have made the astonishing discovery that our spectacular sets of failures at the starting gate had given us a leg up on a lot of "normal" people. We have watched many of them fall hard and stay down when they hit new stress levels and feelings of loss at midlife.

Apparently, they hadn't learned the coping skills and didn't have the self-knowledge we had already been forced to pick up along the way. It is somewhat surprising that many people don't appear to do a self-assessment and then plan their lives as carefully as so many ADDults have tried to do. It seems to be a necessity if one is to survive, but then many of us have had no choice.

A Way Around It—Don't be afraid to take another look at your youthful failures. With your older and wiser eyes, they may take on an entirely different color. In fact, you may end up feeling they were the best thing that ever happened to you.

"There cannot be a crisis next week—my schedule is already full."

—*Henry Kissinger*

No matter how many times we try to organize our lives, hoping to avoid living from one daily crisis to another, we never seem to get it together. We diligently use our personal planners, creating "to-do" lists and scheduling activities, only to discover at the end of the week that we haven't completed a single item on the list. It's particularly frustrating because we *know* we haven't been sitting around doing nothing. Well, okay, maybe sometimes we have to plead guilty on that count. Most of the time, though, we've been overwhelmed by busyness, doing all sorts of things. Too many things, in fact, and that includes feeling anxious and stressed at the frantic pace of our lives. We end up believing that we will never feel in control.

Feeling like miserable failures as our to-do lists grow ever longer, we respond by playing the hated game of "catch-up," often skimping on sleep to borrow those extra hours. The problem is due partly to poor planning and impulsive decisions, but also to our taking on the emergencies of friends and family members. Even when the messes aren't ours to clean up in the first place, we jump into "damage control mode," putting out fires and lurching from one crisis to another.

A Way Around It—Stand in front of a mirror and practice saying *no*, firmly and without hesitation. Or better still, delay your response until you've had time to think things through. Crises are inevitable in your daily life: Handle the ones of your own making but refuse to take on anyone else's.

"If you have the determination to keep everlastingly at it,
you will attain success as well as a nervous breakdown."
—*Herbert V. Prochnow, Sr.*

I'm not really sure what a nervous breakdown is, so I can't
say with certainty that I've ever had one. I can, however,
tell you that I readily identify with the well-known words
on a T-shirt that read: *I have only one nerve left . . . and
you're getting on it!* Having lived with frazzled nerves most
of my life, I feel that I'm an expert on the subject.

Come to think of it, lots of my ADD friends share this
expertise. Not that this is the exclusive purview of
ADDers. Anxiety and frazzled nerves seem to have
become the way of life for many people as they juggle the
details of ever-growing family and work responsibilities.
But the ante is higher for us. As non-ADD peers climb
ever higher on their respective ladders of personal and
professional success, many of us are reaching out for the
bottommost rung, desperately trying to pull ourselves up
to secure a toehold. "Success" becomes our rallying cry as
we push ourselves harder and harder, determined to leave
our failures behind.

Speaking from experience, I can tell you that this system of working oneself to near death worked for me . . .
that is, until I'd exhausted my resources of emotional
and physical energy, crashing and burning for many long
months. What a swell way to experience the joy of
success!

There's nothing wrong with persistence. It's an
admirable quality. But for many ADDers, it becomes plain
old bullheadedness—one of our less than sterling qualities! Under the best circumstances, maintaining a healthy
balance in our lives is difficult. This becomes nearly
impossible when we demand of ourselves nothing less than

perfection. There's no real joy in succeeding when the achievement exacts such a tremendous price—lives thrown into total disequilibrium.

A Way Around It—Take some time for a reality check. Are you being too hard on yourself, working to do something you can't or to be somebody you aren't? If so, use your unique profile of strengths and weaknesses as a guide before taking on new tasks. Head off that impending nervous breakdown . . . and experience the joy of success by staying away from endeavors that tax your personal resources and waste your time. Work instead from your areas of strength, applying your efforts and talents to projects you like and can do well.

—P. R.

"Most of the time I don't have much fun. The rest of the
time I don't have any fun at all."

—*Woody Allen*

How about you? Have you had any fun during the past few
days . . . or weeks . . . or months? If you have to rack your
brain to recall the last time you did something fun or
begin reminiscing about the wonderful summers of your
childhood, it's time for you to make some new memories!
Time? Ah, yes . . . that's both the problem and the solution, isn't it?

In many respects, having ADD makes us less "stress
resistant" than others. We have to deal not only with the
normal wear and tear of daily life but also with our erratic
nervous systems and biochemistry. So, even with the many
demands on our time, it is imperative that we find time to
relax, exercise, and "play."

A Way Around It—Don't think of fun as a luxury that
costs more time than you can afford. Think of it as a
prescription for your improved physical and mental
health. Then brush up on your time management skills,
scrutinizing your daily and weekly schedule, looking for
time wasters. Say *no!* to tasks somebody else thinks you
should do, and delegate household responsibilities whenever possible.

"We experience moments absolutely free from worry.
  These brief respites are called panic."
                                              —*Cullen Hightower*

Did you know that the word *worry* comes from a Greek
word meaning "to divide the mind"? A mind that is
divided is torn, anxious, and incapable of experiencing
peace. How can you ever relax when your mind, without
your permission, constantly ruminates about the obstacles
and problems in your life? Fueled by some added imaginative thinking, your worry can explode into a state of full-
blown panic.

Certainly there are things that merit your attention.
Concern for your family's safety, for example, may moti-
vate you to install smoke detectors in your home. This is
healthy thinking, leading to productive, positive action—
a far cry from the paralyzing counterproductive worry
about things you cannot control.

The problem with worry is that, like a rocking chair, it
gives you something to do but doesn't get you anywhere.
For ADDers, worry can become a habit that frequently
intrudes on our thinking. It is all too easy to get into the
habit of worrying when your life and self are so unpredictable.

A Way Around it—Although it's easy to understand how
and why we develop the worrying habit, using it as a coping strategy is pointless. When you catch yourself slipping
into the worrying mode, practice heading off that potential panic attack through action. If there is something concrete you can do to alleviate your worry, such as installing
those smoke detectors—do it. If there is nothing you can
do, get involved in a mental or physical activity to pull
your focus and concentration away from fruitless worrying.

"For peace of mind, resign as general manager of the
   universe."
                                        —*Larry Eisenberg*

It would be unfair to say that all ADDers are control
freaks. But do you happen to know one or two? A spouse,
perhaps? A child? Yourself? I admit to having a tendency
or two in this regard, as do my ADD spouse and my ADD
son. With three of the four members of the Ramundo family trying to control things, my daughter, Alison, often
assumes the role of peacemaker.

There are several reasons for the ADDer's need for control. Impulsivity makes us jump in, "directing traffic," so to
speak, with little thought to the ensuing confusion created
when someone else is also playing traffic cop. Short fuses
make us respond angrily to decisions made for us with
which we disagree.

Although some ADDers function best with high stimulation, seemingly thriving on chaos, most of us don't.
Rather than gaining a feeling of being in control, driving
people and situations to do things our way typically leaves
us careening out of control, feeling as if we are hanging
precariously over the guardrail at the edge of a precipice.

A Way Around It—Living with frazzled nerves in an environment of constant turmoil is neither healthy nor pleasant. If you would prefer living a more peaceful existence,
you can. The choice is yours to stop trying to do it all, to
stop trying to control every person and every situation
within your little "universe." Just let it go.

"In the old days you waited patiently two hours for a stage-coach but now you gripe if you miss the first section of a revolving door."

— *Anonymous*

It's probably safe to assume that not everyone waited patiently for the stagecoach to arrive! But clearly, the pace of life is considerably faster now than it was in the "old days." It seems that many people these days suffer from a kind of hurry sickness—hurrying to the point that they really do get sick.

We might do better following the example of Mr. William Wellman's homing pigeon that was released in 1939 to compete in a hundred-mile race. It must have glided along at a very leisurely pace, because it didn't return to its Cleveland home until 1949!

If all your time is spent doing, there is no time left for being. You miss the joys of being in the now, which is, you know, the *present*—a gift you owe yourself. It's hard to get more than a passing whiff of the roses if you're charging past them, on a mission to who knows where.

A Way Around It—Take time to just be, putting aside the pressure to accomplish anything. Take just five minutes out of your busy schedule to look at a flower, walk barefoot through a puddle, or watch the leaves blowing in the wind.

"What is my loftiest ambition? I've always wanted to throw an egg into an electric fan."

—*Oliver Herford*

This wouldn't be a terrific response to your prospective boss's inquiry about your long-term career goals, but it does sound like a lot of fun, doesn't it? Sure, it would make quite a mess. But as a strategy for dealing with stress, it has real possibilities, don't you think?

Stress is a serious problem for us ADDers. We are bombarded with sensory overstimulation pouring in through our faulty filtering systems. When we're faced with the added stressors of everyday life, we can be pushed beyond our ability to cope. Although a month's vacation on a deserted island might seem the only remedy, there is a much less expensive way to obtain relief: laughter.

Humor acts as a safety valve, releasing mounting emotional pressures. It can also be good medicine for healing the ailments of the body. Not a bad deal—something that costs nothing and is available in limitless quantities!

A Way Around It—Dream up something outrageous to do. And you don't have to actually throw that egg into an electric fan to enjoy the joke. You can get a lot of humor mileage from a zany idea merely by thinking about it.

"Stress—that confusion created when the mind must override the body's basic desire to choke the living crap out of some idiot who desperately needs it."

—*T-shirt slogan*

Let's be honest. Most of us have made more than an occasional judgment call regarding the idiocy of certain other individuals, secretly relishing the thought of showing them the error of their ways. With great effort, however, we manage to—or ought to!—keep these thoughts to ourselves, refusing to give in to the temptation of acting on them!

Stressors come in many forms, some human, some not. A torrential downpour on the day of the family reunion, a child's fourth detention in a week, a computer that bombs, eating important data—the list of stressors goes on and on. With our low tolerance for frustration, we tend to overreact to these stressors, driving ourselves crazy with feelings of anger and blame. Of course, trying to prevent the circumstances that create stress in your life has the same odds of success as winning the million-dollar lottery. Both are possible, but unlikely.

A Way Around It—Careful planning certainly can help forestall disaster, but it is impossible to control all the life events that create stress. This reality, however, doesn't render you powerless. Although you can't often change the circumstance, you can change your response to it. Faced with a stressful event, you can use this knowledge for self-empowerment. Ask yourself, "Do I want to 'win' or do I want peace of mind?"

10

ADD: A Disorder
or an
ADDed Dimension?

This final section is an unabashed celebration of all the many good things about the ADD heart and mind. Yes, we have annoying habits at times, we make mistakes, and we even drive our own selves crazy. But does that make us nothing but a bunch of losers? Absolutely not! What would the world do without the dreamers, the inventors, the improvisers, and those with enough courage to question the way things have always been done? We are those people, the pioneers who are not afraid to take the risks that can lead to an untried but possibly better solution to a problem.

Many of you may be wondering how this vision relates to the reality of your daily lives. "I'm not an inventor," you may say, "and I don't think I've done anything earthshaking in my life. I'm just an ordinary Joe/Jane, only trying to get through the day most of the time."

And so are we all. The great accomplishments in history were nothing more or less than the rearrangement of ordinary things and ideas. They usually required the efforts of multitudes of people over a long period of time. Then, at the right moment, some lucky person or group of people would have a flash of insight that allowed them to see a common problem from a totally different angle. They were then hailed as great creators, people who were in a class above us ordinary mortals. In reality, they would be nothing without the contributions of many unsung heroes.

We all have the capacity to create; the only difference is that some people are more obvious about it. Practice recognizing and honoring your gifts, even if they are not applauded by the rest of the world—at least, not yet. Keep your big dreams firmly fixed in your mind's eye, but begin with the stuff of your everyday life. If your child-rearing practices are a little unorthodox, but they work, you qualify as a highly creative person. You don't have to hold a patent to be an inventor. Those crazy but useful gadgets you produce to make life easier around the house are the work of an inventive mind. And the idea for a new system for organizing work at the office is just as creative as the efforts of a composer putting the notes together to form a symphony.

"Discovery is seeing what everybody else has seen, and thinking what nobody else has thought."
—*Albert Szent-Gyorgi*

Why does one person look at an event or situation and see what ninety-nine others did not? Some would say intelligence, or sometimes just dumb luck, but perhaps free association is the key. One of the best things about having ADD is our ability to free-fall in a cascade of seemingly unrelated thoughts and ideas. Sometimes those ideas turn out to be just a pile of junk, noise, and mind clutter. At other times, though, we hit pay dirt, a crazy collection of ideas gelling into a useful, unified concept.

Because our brains lack the usual controls on behavior and thinking, we are less likely to put the brakes on our imaginations. Ideas constantly roll around in our heads. It's great fun letting our brains drift from one idea to the next until we come up with some new angle or approach to a situation. When we emerge from a brainstorm with a workable solution to a problem, it is vindication for those times we were scolded for doing too much "wool-gathering."

A Way Around It—Don't be afraid to use free association when you are trying to create something new or solve a problem. It is the key to going beyond the "tried and true" in search of a better way. Do take the time, though, to get rid of the *mind junk*, organizing your thoughts into a coherent presentation before you share them. Even if there is a gem amid that heap of thoughts, it will be overlooked if others have to work too hard to find it.

"A pile of rocks ceases to be a rock pile when somebody contemplates it with the idea of a cathedral in mind."
—*Antoine de Saint-Exupéry*

People with ADD seem to have a knack for envisioning a cathedral when confronted with a pile of rocks, or for creating something wonderful and useful from other people's junk piles. For example, when I was about nine or ten, my ADD friend and I built a series of weird but workable bikes from a pile of discarded parts. One of our creations was a tandem bike with three wheels, made from bolting two bicycle frames together.

As an adult, I still find myself making stuff from something less than the best of materials because I can't afford to do it any other way. It really aggravates me at times—that I'm still hodgepodging many projects because of financial constraints. But when I take the time to really ponder this issue, I realize that the need to make something out of almost nothing has honed my creative skills. I have had to learn to improvise and to change both the direction and vision of many a project, lacking the gear, drill bit, or miter box needed to construct something in a conventional way.

A Way Around It—Don't sit around bemoaning your fate because you are limited to working with what you have. Look at that pile of rocks and allow yourself to envision what it might become. Whether you are doing something concrete, such as building a bike, or a task that is more abstract, view the limits and obstacles as opportunities to exercise creative muscle.

—D. S. L.

"The laziest man I ever met put popcorn in his pancakes so they would turn over by themselves."

—*W. C. Fields*

Why do people put such negative labels on what is, after all, initiative and ingenuity? Was Edison a lazy slob because he refused to accept the inconveniences of candles and gas lamps? Even before he invented the light-bulb, he had no doubt figured out a way to burn candles and lamps more efficiently. Imagine what our lives would be like had he listened to the scoffers of his day, telling him that the status quo was okay.

We are big fans of anything that makes life easier. For example, are you a mediocre cook whose family would starve if it were not for 1) your partner's cooking ability, 2) the prepared foods at the supermarket, and 3) the microwave? If so, take pride in your ability to forage at the store for meals that require little or no preparation but that look and taste like you've spent time slaving away over a hot stove.

A Way Around It—Talk back to those stern and disap-proving voices from the past that scold in your head. The cautions and values handed down through the generations don't necessarily make sense today. Those old Puritans didn't know what they were talking about. If they were here today and could only give themselves permission to question tradition, they might enjoy the improvements that make life a little easier.

"Lord Ronald said nothing; he flung himself from the room, flung himself upon his horse and rode madly off in all directions."

—*Steven Leacock*

The above quote is proof positive that ADD is not just the disease du jour of the nineties. It has been with us for a long time. Perhaps in the old days, however, it was much easier to get away with it. The bold and the restless took off for new frontiers when the itchy "ants in the pants" feeling got too intense.

For example, the United States and Australia were colonized by the misfits of European society. Some were felons or indentured servants looking for a fresh start in life. Others were just unsettled souls thirsting for adventure or the freedom that could not be found where they came from. Then, when the eastern settlements became too domesticated, it was time to "go West," young men and women. Maybe the apparent "explosion" of ADD is related to the fact that there seem to be fewer new worlds for pioneers to conquer.

A Way Around It—Our geographical frontiers may be fewer, but there are still new worlds to conquer. Our imagination is limited only by the fetters we choose to put on it. Look around. There are still improvements to be made in this world we inhabit. Find and fill a need that suits your talents and interests.

"I decided to become an actor because I was failing in
school and I needed the credits."

—*Dustin Hoffman*

Here's a good example of how failure can lead you down a
road that you never envisioned, but that turns out to be
paved with gold. We know that academics are not the be-
all and end-all. There are plenty of excellent students who
are fish out of water once they leave school and try their
hand at real life. And many brilliant entrepreneurs
loathed school. They either dropped out or managed to
pass by, relying on their wits and some luck.

Somehow, though, our school failures haunt us, over-
shadowing our real accomplishments as adults. Those old
report cards stay in our heads, even though they actually
reside in a dusty part of our parents' attic. By the way, who
said that being an actor was a second-class profession anyway? Performers work hard at their craft; the ease with
which they present their finished products is deceiving.

In college, a couple of fraternity jocks joined an acting
class, thinking it would be easy credit. They were aston-
ished and chagrined to find it was harder than any other
course they had taken. Oddly enough, they turned out to
be naturals at acting, especially comedy. Who knows if
they actually did anything with their talent after the
course ended, but at least they discovered a new side of
themselves.

A *Way Around It*—Remind yourself frequently that academic success is highly overrated. It doesn't matter how
well you did in school; consider what you are doing now. It
doesn't have to be anything earthshaking. Just look for
signs that you are working hard, honoring your unique
gifts and talents.

"I have a sixth sense, but not the other five. If I wasn't making money, they'd put me away."

—*Red Skelton*

In a concrete sense, this really rings a bell. ADD wreaks havoc with the brain in varied and subtle ways. Our senses of sight, touch, smell, taste, and hearing are all affected by the disregulation. And since these sensory channels are our means of communication with the real world, it isn't surprising that our connection with it is often full of static. Many of us rely strongly on the psychic and intuitive to guide us. Perhaps a strong sixth sense is a compensatory gift we've been given. Or perhaps we have learned to develop it, as a way to bypass weaknesses. Most likely, it's a bit of both.

A Way Around It—If the disturbances in your sensory pathways are really getting in your way, consider sensory integration training. An occupational therapist is the professional who can help you with this problem. But don't forget that your intuition is a valuable guide. Give it at least the same respect that you give to your other five senses.

"Learn to praise the idiosyncrasies, the eccentricities, the quirks and singularities of others. It will help you to praise your own."

—*John-Roger*

As ADDers, we are both blessed and cursed with an abundance of oddities. There is little danger that any of us will become faceless members of the herd. Even if we strive so hard for normalcy that we cripple our spirits, one of our quirks will eventually surface and blow our cover of conformity. Besides, we don't really think that becoming one of the masses is a great goal in life. So why do we work toward it? The origins of this drive are obvious. Most of us have experienced the tortures of being outcasts, especially as children. But the stakes are different now. They're much more in our favor, because grown-ups are allowed to be a little odd or eccentric. We say, let's learn to honor those idiosyncrasies, the traits that make each of us unique.

A Way Around It—Begin by looking for the endearing aspects of others' quirks. It is generally easier to study behavior as an outside observer, at least in the beginning. If you can learn to accept and appreciate the foibles of others, it may be easier to accept your own.

"There are days when it takes all you've got just to keep up with the losers."

—*Robert Orban*

Too many of us think of ourselves as less than losers. But think again. What do we mean by winners and losers anyway? That person you admire with a great career and lots of money may be a nasty tyrant at home. He may end life alone and terrified, realizing too late that you really "can't take it with you." The woman who seems to have a perfectly organized life, with husband, home, work, and children all in order, may be covering up a joyless, soulless existence. Perhaps we ADDers don't always "climb the ladder of success" as high or as fast as we're supposed to—at least according to societal expectations. But we aren't likely to be accused of lacking passion, humor, or a sense of wonder. We are well equipped to notice and receive the gifts of the spirit.

A Way Around It—Fashion another yardstick for measuring success: your personal definition of winning. We'll give you the Kelly/Ramundo definition from *You Mean I'm Not Lazy, Stupid or Crazy?!* for starters: "Success is achieved when you figure out what you were born to do and fashion a lifestyle that enables you to do it."

"Why can't we sell parents on the 'possibility of finding a genius in your child' instead of identifying a potential felon, drug addict, alcoholic, future divorcée, and dunce?"

—*Robin Hood Brians*

Unfortunately, it seems that the media tend to focus on the cases where people with ADD get into trouble with the law or screw up in some fashion. It's the ratings game, folks. As long as people want to watch that stuff, the people who earn their living selling it will continue to produce the sensational programs.

We don't mean to paint a totally gloomy picture, however. There are those in the media who buck the trends, the bottom line notwithstanding. We have personally had the opportunity to participate in some excellent programs, both on radio and television. These were balanced programs that presented ADDers in a more positive light. They told stories of successful people with ADD and of people with ADD who struggle but still manage to contribute to their communities. These are the stories that need more exposure.

A *Way Around It*—It is possible to do something about the way we are portrayed in the media. And you don't have to be a network executive to have an impact, either. For example, if enough people protest the sensational shows, writing to express their wishes regarding future media coverage, we will eventually be heard.

"I don't use any method. I'm from the let's pretend school of acting."
—*Harrison Ford*

Don't you wish more people would subscribe to this school—for a lot of things in life. In our society, we've forgotten our childhoods, our days of make-believe and playfulness. We have even regimented our children's lives, with full schedules of sports and lessons. Instead of socializing ourselves, we take classes to learn sophisticated techniques for doing various activities. Usually, we would have been better off on our own because the methods often get in the way.

We become so busy concentrating on the "how" of doing something that we forget its purpose. In the process, we forget to have fun, and the activity loses all its magic. You know how it works. We take up golf or tennis because we think it will be fun. And before we know it, we are all caught up in concerns about our game. How well are we doing? Is this the proper way to do it? In no time at all, the game becomes a deadly serious chore if you don't watch out.

A Way Around It—Give yourself permission to loosen up and allow your playful side to be a driving force in your activities. Perhaps golf or tennis are not good choices for leisure time activities if the rest of your life is highly structured, unless you can play with people who don't take the whole thing so darn seriously. Kate and Peggy play tennis with a group of women we laughingly refer to as the LD league. Most of us actually do have learning disabilities, but some of us are pretty good anyway. The main thing is that we are more interested in having a good time, in sometimes fudging the rules and trading jokes over the net, than we are in actually winning.

"I just invent, then wait until man comes around to needing what I've invented."

—R. Buckminster Fuller

A futuristic vision often comes with the ADD territory.
We are long on imagination, a characteristic that can take
us on fantastic voyages where no one else has gone before.
But what can we do when the world is not ready for our
art, or our new product, or that idea that will revolutionize
our field?

Well, this is an area where we can practice patience
while we wait for the demand to catch up to the supply.
Kate and Peggy had to deal with this problem during the
process of creating *You Mean I'm Not Lazy, Stupid or
Crazy?!* Here was this great idea that we were convinced
would translate into a surefire hit. Nobody had written a
self-help book for ADD adults yet, and we knew that we
could do the job. Few people had heard about adult ADD
then, but we figured it would be big news by the time the
manuscript was completed.

To our chagrin, it didn't happen in quite that way. Publishers initially rejected our proposals, saying they didn't
think there would be a big enough market for the book. It
was finally self-published and then purchased by a major
publisher. But the process took years, many more than
either of us had bargained for.

A Way Around It—Don't expect the world to jump up
and down the first time you present your creations and
ideas, but don't give up either. It will always take longer
than you think it will. In the meantime, you will be more
content if you have more than one iron in the fire. It is
much easier to wait when you have other projects to work
on and other means of generating income.

"I used to think it was the people who were weird who were weird, but then I figured out that it was the people who thought they were weird, who were weird."
—*Paul McCartney*

Paul McCartney once said that the album that influenced him the greatest as a developing musician was the Beach Boys' *Smiley Smile*, the most experimental recording the Beach Boys had done up to that time. In it they tried all sorts of unusual recording techniques, such as singing in an empty swimming pool because they liked the acoustics. Some might label their methods "weird," but we would say that those people probably suffer from the sour grapes syndrome, and would be more than happy to engage in "weird" behavior of their own if it would net them multi-million-dollar record contracts.

People are all too eager to classify unconventional ADD behavior as weirdness and then to dismiss us on that basis. Never mind that our strange and circuitous ways of getting things done often produce good results. "They" conveniently forget that most of the great minds in history were quirky and eccentric, to say the least. Einstein, Edison, and Buckminister Fuller did not have personalities that blended into the crowd, but one would be a fool to discount their contributions to society.

A Way Around It—When someone gives you that "boy, are you strange" look, consider it a compliment. It is a testimony to your uniqueness. People who look down their noses at anything out of the ordinary are to be pitied rather than censured, for they suffer under the constraints of a narrow mind.

"Not to dream boldly may turn out to be simply irresponsible."

—George Leonard

Irresponsible. That hated word many of us with ADD have heard our whole lives. As children, we were called irresponsible when we didn't do our chores correctly or didn't "try hard enough" to complete school work. Of course, much of this criticism was heaped on us as we daydreamed, our creative minds taking us on wonderful journeys, sometimes solving all kinds of interesting problems.

Since our performance didn't measure up to expectations, we must have been lazy, irresponsible creatures, right? Perhaps not. Despite dire predictions about our future endeavors, many of us managed to nurture our quirky thinking style, finding our niche in adulthood. Perhaps you're still struggling to discover the best use of creative talents unappreciated during your childhood. In any case, we'd like to offer a different perspective on what it means to be irresponsible. To have gifts of imagination and minds that leap to make connections where there seemingly aren't any, but fail to use them—wouldn't that be the worst kind of irresponsibility?

A Way Around It—Unless you've found a job that pays you for your ideas and ability to "possibilitize," you'll have to continue reining in your wandering thoughts at work. Daydreaming doesn't often pay the bills! But don't squelch your random thoughts too much. At the very least, make time to engage in creative endeavors. Allow yourself the luxury of giving free flight to your imagination and pursuing your boldest of dreams. Who knows, those dreams might just evolve into a "real" job!

"Our ordinary mind always tries to persuade us that we are nothing but acorns and that our greatest happiness will be to become bigger, fatter, shinier acorns; but that is of interest only to pigs. Our faith gives us knowledge of something much better: that we can become oak trees.

—*E. F. Schumacher*

It's so easy for us to fall in the trough and wallow in self-pity. Oh, poor me: I didn't ask to be born with ADD; I didn't ask for all the criticism heaped on me when I was growing up. We don't just stop at the pity party, either. We decide that somebody has to be held responsible for all the unfairness in our lives, so we start rounding up a group of likely suspects. We wouldn't have any of these problems if it weren't for this person or that circumstance, would we?

The next step we take is looking for a quick fix. An easy solution. Of course, the world we live in is plastered with advertising hype promising easy answers to both the difficult and the inconsequential dilemmas of daily life. Feeling left out from the crowd? Wear XYZ Jeans for Instant Popularity! . . . Housework got you down? Try the new Home Riding Vacuum Cleaner! If you stop to reflect on this thinking, you will quickly realize that it effectively renders you powerless. It is nothing more than looking to the past to assign blame and looking to the future to find the magical fix. This "smoke-screen" thinking is counterproductive, obscuring and distorting the reality of your "now" and your awareness of the progress you've already made.

A Way Around It—Don't settle for less than what you really desire, wasting your energy bemoaning your sorry state, blaming somebody else for it, and hunting for the key to your instant success. With these thoughts taking up space in your brain, there isn't any room for the kind of thinking that can actually lead you to accomplish something! The solutions for personal growth aren't somewhere out there. They're in here, within your hopes, dreams, and goals. Be mindful of your unique qualities now while visualizing the "you" you want to work toward becoming.

"A lot of people told me I was never going to be anybody. But here I am."

—*Rodney A. Grant*

Do you have irresistible urges to go back to your old high school and show those people that they were wrong? Predictions made then are, more times than not, wrong. The "Person Most Likely to Succeed" goes to Harvard for a semester and flunks out, unable to deal with the social pressures of college life. The last you heard about him, he was spending his days lying on the couch reading comic books. And the class nerd got it together and made a big splash in the music business. Perhaps you were that hapless student labeled the "Class Nerd." Many of us were. We have struggled since then to make something of ourselves.

Who were those people who told you that you would never amount to anything? Was it your boring history teacher, the one who sat at his desk every day, reading out of his beloved old college textbook to his comatose class? Or maybe it was that short-tempered music teacher—the frustrated performing artist—who expected you to demonstrate the brilliance she never had? And let's not forget the kids from the "In" group who taunted you. Do you really still care what those people thought?

A Way Around It—The urge to go back there and show 'em they were wrong is powerful, isn't it? But why waste your time even thinking about those nagging voices of critical people from your past? If it helps, talk back to those voices in the privacy of your mind, clearing out the images of those naysayers and making room for thoughts of your successes.

Resources for
Adults with ADD

BOOKS

GENERAL

ADD Success Stories: A Guide to Fulfillment for Families with Attention Deficit Disorder
Thom Hartmann
Grass Valley, Calif.: Underwood Press, 1995
1-887424-03-2

Answers to Distraction: The Authors of Driven to Distraction Respond to the Most Frequently Asked Questions about Attention Deficit Disorder
Edward M. Hallowell, M.D., and John J. Ratey, M.D.
New York: Pantheon, 1994
0-679-43973-0

Attention Deficit Disorder: A Different Perception: New Ways to Work with Attention Deficit Disorder at Home, Work, and School
Thom Hartmann
Grass Valley, Calif.: Underwood-Miller, 1993
0-88733-156-4

Attention Deficit Disorder in Adults: A Comprehensive Guide to Research, Diagnosis, Treatment
Edited by Kathleen G. Nadeau, Ph.D.
New York: Brunner/Mazel Publishers, 1995
0-87630-760-8

Attention Deficit Disorder in Adults: Practical Help for Sufferers and Their Spouses
Lynn Weiss
Dallas: Taylor Publishing, 1994
0-87833-779-2

Attention-Deficit Hyperactivity Disorder in Adults
Paul H. Wender, M.D.
New York: Oxford University Press, 1995
0-19-509227-9

Driven to Distraction: Recognizing and Coping with Attention Deficit Disorder from Childhood through Adulthood
Edward M. Hallowell, M.D., and John J. Ratey, M.D.
New York: Fireside, 1994
0-679-42177-7

The Link Between ADD and Addiction
Wendy Richardson, M.A.
Colorado Springs: Pinon Press, 1997

Out of Chaos: Understanding and Managing A.D.D. and Its Relationship to Modern Stress
Sanjay Jasuja, M.D.
Palo Alto, Calif.: Esteem House, 1995
0-9647153-0-9

Think Fast—The ADD Experience: CompuServe's Attention Deficit Disorder Forum
Thom Hartmann and Janie Bowman with Susan Burgess
Grass Valley, Calif.: Underwood Press, 1996
1-887424-08-3

Women with Attention Deficit Disorder: Embracing Disorganization at Home and in the Workplace
Sari Solden, MS, MFCC
Grass Valley, Calif.: Underwood Books, 1995
1-887424-05-9

You Mean I'm Not Lazy, Stupid or Crazy?! A Self-Help Book for Adults with Attention Deficit Disorder
Kate Kelly and Peggy Ramundo
New York: Fireside, 1995
0-684-80116-7

PARENTING

Beyond Ritalin: Facts about Medication and Other Strategies for Helping Children, Adolescents, and Adults with Attention Deficit Disorders
Stephen W. Garber, Ph.D., Marianne Daniels Garber, Ph.D., and Robyn Freedman Spizman
New York: Villard, 1996
0-679-45018-1

Children with Tourette Syndrome: A Parent's Guide
Edited by Tracy Haerle
Rockville, Md.: Woodbine House, 1992
0-933149-44-1

The Misunderstood Child: A Guide for Parents of Children with Learning Disabilities, 2nd Edition
Larry B. Silver, M.D.
Blue Ridge Summit, Pa.: Tab Books, 1992
0-8306-2954-8

No One to Play With: The Social Side of Learning Disabilities
Betty B. Osman and Henriette Blinder
Novato, Calif.: Academic Therapy Publications, 1982
0-87879-687-8

Scoutmaster's Guide to ADD: For Adults Working with Attention Deficit Disorder in Scouting and Other Youth Activities
D. Steven Ledingham
Tucson, Ariz.: Positive People Press, 1994
(520) 749-5465

Taming the Dragons: Real Help for Real School Problems
Susan Setley, M.Sp.Ed.
St. Louis: Starfish Publishing, 1995
1-886243-04-2
(314) 367-9611

Why Johnny Can't Concentrate: Coping with Attention Deficit Problems
Robert A. Moss, M.D., with Helen Huff Dunlap
New York: Bantam, 1990
0-553-34968-6

You and Your ADD Child: How to Understand and Help Kids with Attention Deficit Disorder
Paul Warren, M.D., and Jody Capehart, M. Ed.
Nashville: Thomas Nelson, 1995
0-7852-7895-8

Your Hyperactive Child: A Parent's Guide to Coping
with Attention Deficit Disorder
Barbara Ingersoll, Ph.D.
New York: Doubleday, 1988
0-385-24070-8

THE WORKPLACE

Attention Deficit Disorder and the Law
Peter S. Latham, J.D., and Patricia H. Latham, J.D.
Washington, D.C.: JKL Communications, 1993
1-883560-00-4

Focus Your Energy: Hunting for Success in Business
with Attention Deficit Disorder
Thom Hartmann
New York: Pocket Books, 1994
0-671-5189-2

Succeeding in the Workplace
Peter S. Latham, J.D., and Patricia H. Latham, J.D.
Washington, D.C.: JKL Communications, 1994
1-883560-03-9

RELATIONSHIPS

Honey, Are You Listening? How Attention Deficit Disor-
der Could Be Affecting Your Marriage
Rick Fowler, Ph.D., and Jerilyn Fowler
Nashville: Thomas Nelson, 1995
0-8407-7710-8

Medications for Attention Disorders (ADHD/ADD) and Related Medical Problems (Tourette's Syndrome, Sleep Apnea, Seizure Disorders)
Edna D. Copeland, Ph.D., with Stephen C. Copps, M.D.
New York: Specialty Press, 1995
1-886941-00-9
<u>LIFE SKILLS</u>

A.D.D. and Success: Discover Your A.D.D. Power . . . Turn Your Daydreams into Reality
Marilyn Kroplick, M.D.
Los Angeles: Learning Annex, 1996

The ASK Guide to ADD Self-Help Groups
D. Steven Ledingham and Reed Robertson
Tucson, Ariz.: Positive People Press, 1995
1-890734-02-0

The Attention Deficit Disorder in Adults Workbook
Lynn Weiss
Dallas: Taylor Publishing, 1994
0-878-33850-0

Square Peg in a Round Hole: Coping with Learning Differences at Home, in School, and at Work
Jimmie Shreve, PE
San Diego: Square Peg Enterprises, 1993
0-963-9421-0-7

The Twelve Steps: A Key to Living with Attention Deficit Disorder Friends in Recovery
San Diego: RPI Publishing, 1996
0-941405-34-6

Attention Deficit Disorder Association (ADDA)
9930 Johnny Cake Ridge Road, Suite 3E
Mentor, OH 44060
or
P.O. Box 972
Mentor, OH 44061
(800) 487-2282/(216) 350-9595

**Attention Deficit Disorder Association, Southern
    Region**
12345 Jones Road, Suite 287
Houston, TX 77070
(281) 955-3720

**Children and Adults with Attention Deficit Disorders
    (CHADD)**
CHADD National Headquarters
499 NW 70th Avenue, Suite 308
Plantation, FL 33317
(305) 587-3700

Learning Disabilities Association (LDA)
4156 Library Road
Pittsburgh, PA 15234
(412) 341-1515

The Orton Dyslexia Society
Chester Building #382
8600 La Salle Road
Baltimore, MD 21204
(301) 296-0232

The REBUS Institute
1499 Old Bayshore Highway, Suite 146
Burlingame, CA 94010
(415) 697-7424

Tourette Syndrome Association, Inc.
42-40 Bell Boulevard
Bayside, NY 11361
(718) 224-1136

NEWSLETTERS

ADD ONS
(A "paper support group" for people living with ADD)
P.O. Box 675
Frankfort, IL 60423

ADDult News
c/o Mary Jane Johnson
ADDult Support Network
2620 Ivy Place
Toledo, OH 43613

CHADDER Box, CHADDER, and *ATTENTION!*
CHADD National Headquarters
499 NW 70th Avenue, Suite 308
Plantation, FL 33317
FOCUS
ADDA (National Attention Deficit Disorder Association)
P.O. Box 972
Mentor, OH 44061

With the explosive development of Internet resources, the way we locate and distribute information has undergone many significant changes. While books and news media remain viable information resources, the Internet has given many of us access to a "virtual encyclopedia" that is constantly being updated.

The Internet allows nearly anyone with a computer to make information publicly available. For ADDers this means more people can share their personal stories and other information much more easily, and we can read about, share in, and learn from their experiences. The amount of information on the Internet is simply amazing, and I strongly encourage our readers to learn how to tap into this evolving resource.

All information on the Internet is located on "pages," which are located by the computer through "hyperlinks" or "uniform resource locators" (URLs). The following list contains information about those ADD-related "pages" that are, in my experience, the most powerful sources of ADD information on the Net. Many e-mail service providers can give you access to the Internet for a reasonable basic monthly fee. Support groups who have even one member with Net access can collect Internet inf ormation and print it to share with other group members. I believe every ADD support group should gain access to the Net.

To use a hyperlink, you must enter the information *exactly as it is shown*. The beginning of *all hyperlinks* to Net "pages" is http://www. It must be all lowercase! This tells the computer that this is a link to a World Wide Web page, and the rest of the information tells the computer exactly where the page is located. If you have a problem, there is a good chance that you entered the hyperlink incorrectly. Simply try it again. I hope you enjoy cruising the Internet.

—D. S. L.

ADDA (the Attention Deficit Disorder Association)
http://www.azstarnet.com/~sled

This is the World Wide Web site of the National Attention Deficit Disorder Association. This is fast becoming a "must see" site for ADD adults. Also a great source of information on the annual ADDA conference.

ADDNET
gopher://moe.coe.uga.edu:70/11/ITN: Interactive Teaching Network of UGA/ADDNET

Many good articles on ADD intervention techniques, especially in education. Type the address into your Web browser, *exactly* as it is written. This will let you select articles to save on your computer.

ADD News for Christian Families
http://members.aol.com/addnews/index.html

ADD News is the only publication that is written by Christians for Christians, and devoted entirely to Attention Deficit Disorder and related topics. Lots of good information for anyone with ADD.

ADD on AOL
http://members.aol.com/JimAMS/addonaol7.html

This is a very active Web site on America On-Line. Frequently updated and filled with exciting and helpful information for adults, parents, and children with ADD.

ADDult Recovery
http://www.signasoft.com/add/
A site for ADDults interested in using a twelve-step approach in creating success in their lives. Created and maintained by an ADDult.

ADD WebNet
http://members.aol.com/addwebnet/index.html
Personal stories of parents who are educating and raising children with ADD; professionals sharing some of their hard-won knowledge about treating ADD; everything from poetry to artwork by ADD adults. The ADD WebNet is as varied and creative as the individuals who have volunteered their time to build it.

Americans with Disabilities Act Document Center
http://www.ed.gov/offices/OSERS/OSEP/osep.html
Lots of information on legal issues for ADDers.

ASK about ADD (Adults Seeking Knowledge about ADD)
http://www.azstarnet.com/~ask
Steven Ledingham, the cofounder of the original site for the National Attention Deficit Disorder Association, has created a site celebrating the excitement and positives of the ADD experience. In Steven's own words it's not ADD, its B.I.T.S. (Brilliant Interrupted Thinking Stuff).

He maintains a large listing of ADD-related hyperlinks.

Brandi Valentine's Site
http://www.ns.net/users/BrandiV/

This site is one of the earliest sites for ADD and continues to get better and better. A must-visit site!

Canadian Professionals' ADD Centre
http://www.usask.ca/psychiatry/CPADDC.html

An area designed for Canadian teachers, counselors, psychologists, nurses, physicians (including pediatricians), neurologists, family physicians, psychiatrists, and anyone else with a professional interest in assisting people with ADD and their families.

CHADD (Children and Adults with Attention Deficit Disorders)
http://www.chadd.org/

A nonprofit parent-based organization formed to better the lives of individuals with attention deficit disorders and those who care for them. The largest organization of its type in the world.

International Coach Federation
http://www.coachu.com/

Everything about ADD coaching.

Another ADD coaching site that's worth checking out is http://web.addcoach.com/p.

Meng Wong's ADD Archive
http://www.seas.upenn.edu/~mengwong/add/

No list would be complete without Meng Wong's ADD site. This was one of the first sites I ever visited in my search for ADD information.